Condemned

Condemned

Mark Rowan

MONARCH
BOOKS
Oxford, UK & Grand Rapids, Michigan, USA

First published in the UK in 2007 by Monarch Books
(a publishing imprint of Lion Hudson plc),
Mayfield House, 256 Banbury Road, Oxford, OX2 7DH.
Tel: +44 (0) 1865 302750   Fax: +44 (0) 1865 302757
Email: monarch@lionhudson.com
www.lionhudson.com

ISBN 978 1 85424 812 1 (UK)
ISBN 978 0 8254 6166 8

Distributed by:
UK: Marston Book Services Ltd, PO Box 269,
Abingdon, Oxon OX14 4YN
US: Kregel Publications, PO Box 2607,
Grand Rapids, Michigan 49501

British Library Cataloguing Data
A catalogue record for this book is available
from the British Library.

Certain names have been changed in this book
to protect individual's identities where appropriate.

Book design and production for the publishers by New Wine Press
Typeset by CRB Associates, Reepham, Norfolk
Cover design by CCD, www.ccdgroup.co.uk
Cover photography by Mark Theisinger, www.marktheisinger.com
Printed in Malta

The text paper used in this book has been made from wood independently
certified as having come from sustainable forests.

Dedication

To Andrea, my wife –
an extraordinary woman of faith

Acknowledgements

My sincere thanks go to John and Andrene Partington for their friendship and for believing in me and helping me when it mattered the most.

To Bill Hill and Martin Kiddle, my prison chaplains, for their immeasurable support and friendship.

A big thank you to Shane and Lorraine Dean for being great friends and for encouraging me to write my story in the first place. May many lives be touched and changed by reading this book!

Prologue:
A Thug Is Born

I had lost it. The drugs were beating through my veins. Evil possessed me. I screamed, "Come on!" and "Kill!" as I charged at the windows to head butt them through. Blood flowed from my wounds, but I felt absolutely no pain. It didn't bother me. I was drug-crazed, rebellious and out of control. I didn't give a damn what happened to me.

The riot squad, armed with truncheons and shields, queued up outside the prison's TV room. This only fuelled my frenzy all the more. Dozens of us inmates, violent, fuelled by substance abuse and in the mood to inflict some serious damage smashed everything inside the room to high heaven. We were utterly intent on destruction and, as usual, I led the way. I had a two-inch wide gash on my forehead and was losing a lot of blood. I ripped off my T-shirt and tied it around my head.

My mates flicked on their gas lighters. We had totally trashed the room. We laughed and smoked joints to celebrate our success. Nothing made me happier than being bad. Violence and crime gave me my purpose in life. As one of the most feared gang leaders in Yorkshire, my life consisted of a daily dice with evil. Maybe the sexual and physical abuse I'd suffered as a kid had caused me to turn out this way? Perhaps it was the lack of love. Maybe it was some other event that sparked off the endlessly destructive cycle my life was caught in. Whatever it was, I was now thoroughly hooked on pursuing evil. I didn't care who got hurt, maimed, abused or even killed along the way – as long as I got what I wanted.

At that time I supposed that most people heading towards their thirties were preparing to start a family or were entering the most prosperous part of their career. Such lives were irrelevant to me. All I knew was that I was on a fast-track route to destruction, perhaps even death. There were endless rounds of crack, heroin and other drugs. I had used and abused women, smashed heads in – sometimes to protect my territory and sometimes just because someone got in my way – and I had toured the prisons like some people tour historic towns. I had seen things that are usually reserved for seedy, late-night cable channel B-movies.

I had heard that people like me got started because of what they call a "dysfunctional background". All I knew was that my life was a sad, depressing, meaningless mess. My mum gave birth to all eight pounds of me in November 1970. I doubt that I was planned. Walkley Terrace, Yorkshire, wasn't the best place to start off either. Many a home will set the scene for the life of a famous musician, a high-flying lawyer or a professional politician. Mine was the breeding ground for a violent thug.

Chapter 1

My earliest childhood memories date back to 1974 when I was four years old. We lived in a small house on Walkley Terrace in a little town called Heckmondwike in West Yorkshire, around eight miles south of Leeds. It was a rough area. There was me, my mother and my real father, Billy – a man who had (and still has to this day) a reputation for violence, and who had spent many years in and out of prison, mainly for fighting and breaking and entering. His nickname was "Streetfighter Billy". He loved hunting – rabbits, foxes, badgers, anything – and all his life was obsessed with his ferrets, his dogs and his guns. He was well known to the police throughout Yorkshire. Whenever my dad was in jail, which was regularly, my mother or grandma would take me, along with my brother Danny, to visit him.

In our family poverty was a way of life and a constant theme for our existence. My mother would walk miles every morning with Danny and me in a pram to Gran's house for breakfast, because there was never any food in the cupboards at home. One day Dad came home drunk. I remember it so vividly. He went berserk and started shouting at Mum because the only thing to eat in the whole house was a single Fray Bentos pie in a metal tin. Even though the rest of us were starving he began to open it to give it to his precious dogs to eat. Mum went mental because he was going to waste the only bit of food we had on his dogs. In a rage he turned and hurled the half-opened can with its jagged edge in her direction. It stuck fast in the door frame not far from me – the frightened, bewildered onlooker who was beginning to learn from this "role model", soaking the visual information up like a sponge.

I can't recall exactly when, but Mum divorced Dad at some point. All I remember is that suddenly Danny, my other brother Wayne and I spent a lot of time with our grandma and aunt. They didn't seem to like my mum very much, but us boys were at our happiest when we were with our Gran.

By the age of seven our family had moved to the Windy-bank Estate, Hightown, a burgeoning council estate just out of Cleckheaton that was notorious in the area. It had an infamous reputation with all the locals and especially the police who, by necessity, visited it often. As council estates go it was the pits – the worst of the worse. Run down, neglected and a hotbed of criminal activity. It was the sort of place where everyone knew, or at least knew *about*, everyone else; and if they didn't know you, you were a suspect. I don't remember why or how we got there, but there we were – my mother, my two brothers and me in a three-bedroom council house.

We hadn't lived in Hightown long before my mum began to take us frequently to visit a man who lived in another of the houses on the estate. He was the local window cleaner and had three sons himself. In due course he and my mum got

12

together and he moved, three sons and all, into our cramped little house. Suddenly, in addition to me, Danny and Wayne, there were three more boys – Alan, Tony and another Danny. Then there was this man who seemed to be trying to take the place of my dad. I didn't like it and it was intimidating for a young boy. Eight people crammed into a tiny three-bedroom house. I found it all really confusing and just couldn't understand what was going on. We had two sets of bunk beds in one room, my mum and the window cleaner in the next room, and another bunk bed in the smallest bedroom. Although my memory of it is hazy, I know that during this time I was sexually abused by someone in the house and this led to me having an unusual obsession with my sexual organs. I honestly don't know who my abuser was; I buried the event deep down within me where it was to stay for many, many years and tried not to think about it.

The window cleaner, Allan senior, became my stepfather. Looking back you can only be amazed at the choices people make in life. Despite her experiences with my father, my mum had somehow chosen another man who was a violent alcoholic. Normal service was resumed. We all had no choice but to get on with life and survive as best we could. I remember that every meal time, us six boys would have to sit around a little bench table in the kitchen, squashed together elbow to elbow, while Allan sat in the living room with his meal on his lap, watching the TV. When we had finished our meal we had to shout from the kitchen, "Excuse me, please may I leave the table?" Typically, this first plea elicited no response. Louder we would shout, "Excuse me sir, please may I leave the table?" Sometimes the gruff response would be, "No, wait" for no discernable reason and other times it would be a sullen, "Yes".

My mother became pregnant by Allan and gave birth to another boy, Dean. Yet another body to fill up our impossibly cramped living space and another mouth to feed. Yet Allan spent a great deal of his time down at the local pub. On a typical evening my mum would go and join him later in the evening and Danny, the eldest of Allan's boys, would baby sit the rest of us, if you could call it that. It was usually an opportunity to watch something scary on the TV like *Tales of the Unexpected*. Most nights when Mum and Allan returned from the pub there would be shouting, screaming and it would invariably end with my mum being beaten. We were all terrified by this. Mum suffered a catalogue of injuries: black eyes and bruises were the norm, but on one occasion a broken arm. No one ever did anything to stop it.

Wayne and I were seen as the troublemakers in Allan's eyes. Always in trouble, always doing something wrong. Whenever we crossed him or were caught doing something we shouldn't, Allan would put us, kicking and screaming in protest, over his knee and whack us with a leather belt with a heavy buckle. He showed no mercy, even if it was a trivial misdemeanour and sometimes though we'd done nothing other than act like normal, boisterous young lads. If the belt wasn't handy at the scene of our "crime" then he would use his fists and physically beat us. He saw it as disciplining us and teaching us how to behave through the use of pain. As a young kid I saw it as sheer evil bullying and way over the top.

All the good memories I have of those early years at Windybank are not from home but from my experiences on the streets as part of various gangs. Groups of us would gather on the street corners and go looking to do some mischief. One favourite pastime was balancing milk bottles on people's door handles and then knocking on the door so that the bottle would smash at their feet when they answered. Another was going down to the railway tracks and throwing stones at the windows of the factory opposite, aiming to smash as many as possible before the workers inside were on to us. We also thought it was amusing to intimidate the residents of an old people's housing complex. We would kick people's front doors and throw stones at their windows until someone had the bottle to come out and chase us off. When they did we would eventually retreat, but not without yelling abuse at them as we went. On one occasion a guy appeared from nowhere and chased us wielding a large spanner.

Why did we do this? Why do kids set out to inflict misery on others? There must be numerous reasons and I can only speak for myself and my mates. We were bored kids who didn't want to go back home to witness or be a part of the abuse that we knew was an inevitable part of life. If not abuse then parental disinterest and neglect at best. As a result we ended up not only causing trouble and terrorising the local residents, but experimenting with substance abuse to get high – anything that would numb the senses and provide a momentary respite from the awful daily reality. Whenever I could I would get hold of a can of gas. I would press it against my teeth, inhaling the fumes, and lie on the ground hallucinating until I had drained the can. Inhaling gas was just the beginning of what would become a dark descent into the world of drug abuse. There would be more dangerous substances, much greater highs and the subsequent, devastating lows. I had no idea at that point what it could or would lead to.

Soon petty theft became a regular part of my day. The poverty of our family was a factor, of course – we had virtually nothing – but also the boredom, the frustration of my existence and the lack of a positive parental role model were factors. I began by stealing small items from local shops: sweets, pies and other small things. If ever my mum needed a pint of milk in the morning I would volunteer to go and get it. Usually I would keep the money and simply steal a pint off someone else's doorstep.

The beatings at home were becoming more regular and it seemed that it was always Wayne and me who bore the brunt of Allan's anger. Wayne spent so much time in his bedroom, not allowed out, that he became known as "the boy in the window" by people who lived on our street. My brother Danny seemed to escape the beatings. He had his head screwed on a little better than Wayne and I did, and always managed to keep a low profile. I can't recall Allan ever laying a hand on any of his own three sons. As I grew older I became fascinated with the topic of war and all its trappings: tanks, bombs, weapons of every description. One of my more innocuous pastimes was going down the cunnies (fields) with my friends and looking for the bones of soldiers in the old air-raid shelters. We thought we might find something, but of course, we never did! I collected war magazines and old medals whenever I could get them and I dreamed about being a soldier. I managed to acquire my first two knives – one a Ghurkha knife and the other a Chinese knife – and keep them hidden.

People on the estate called me "Super Kid". I had a growing reputation for performing dangerous stunts and managing to survive relatively unscathed. I was a good BMXer and would set out to do crazy stunts that none of the other kids dared attempt. I wanted to prove to everyone that I was fearless. I also had a kind of self-destructive streak developing that said, "I'm not afraid of anyone or anything. I just don't care." Once

I went to the local park and put a ramp up against the crossbar of the football goalposts. You can imagine it was fairly steep. Thinking back I'm surprised I didn't just smash right through the middle of it, never mind go up it. I charged at that ramp, peddling like crazy, made the top and shot into the air above the posts. I had one of those slow motion moments that people talk about as I was temporarily suspended in mid-air enjoying the glory of other's amazement and then I came crashing down to earth. Of course, I broke my bike, but I revelled in my "Super Kid" title and was determined to do ever more outrageous stunts to prove my ownership of it whenever I could.

School was a waste of time as far as I was concerned. The teachers couldn't control me and before long I was playing truant most of the time. My first criminal offence was to take an axe to a local park with a friend and chop up the park's wooden swings and benches. I wasn't yet thirteen years old, but I was arrested and given a conditional discharge for criminal damage. By this time I had also burgled a house on our street. Although I only took some small change, ate some of their food and generally made a mess there, I knew it was in me to pursue this more seriously. I knew the people I had burgled and actually chatted to them afterwards with no conscience about the fact that I had ripped them off and they had no idea it was me. On another occasion I remember a gang of us stole a fire extinguisher from a factory and carried it back to our estate. We were all gathered outside the shops when the police came. I aimed the fire extinguisher at the police but I didn't have the guts to set it off at that stage.

Thus began a cycle of committing crimes and being appre-hended by the police. As the years wore on the crimes would become bigger and the penalties for being caught greater. But for now it was more of a cat and mouse game. If I thought the police were on to me for something I'd done I would run away from home – just head off not knowing where I was going, full of hate and resentment for my dysfunctional family and home life and determined never to go back. But the police would always find me, often miles from home, and take me back.

One such excursion took place when my friend, Paul, and I were hanging around near an amusement arcade in the town. We were bored, kicking around trying to stay out of the way of the police when we saw a van pull up outside the building. A man got out and carried two heavy-looking bags inside. The fact that the bags were making a chinking sound left nothing to the imagination. It was money!

Foolishly, the guy didn't lock his van, so as soon as he disappeared into the building we ran over, opened the door and managed to grab two or three more of the bags that were sitting inside. We legged it as fast as we could away from the scene of the crime. Our pulses were racing and hearts pounding as we raced towards the fields with money spilling out everywhere. When we were sure we were safe we headed over to a den we'd where we wouldn't be disturbed and could examine our loot more closely. We emptied the contents of the bags all over the floor and shared out equally what was, to us, a massive amount of money. Each of us ended up with our own carrier bag full of cash in coins. Now we thought about what to do with it.

Going from having no money to what seemed like a small fortune our plans were ambitious to say the least. We decided we would run away to nearby Bradford. When we got there the first thing we did was walk into the nearest electronics store and buy ourselves identical Walkmans.

They must have thought we'd been saving our pocket money for years to produce so much change, but we thought we were millionaires! Next we went to a local restaurant and ordered a huge meal. Here we were treated with a good deal more suspicion by the restaurant staff than we'd experienced buying the Walkmans. Naturally, they were wondering how this couple of scruffy looking lads were going to pay their bill. At the end of the meal we both reached into our carrier bags and paid with a mountain of change!

Short sighted and naive, Paul and I made a pact that we would never go home again. We enjoyed having money, but we relished our freedom all the more. Sadly, that night the police caught us while we were roaming the streets of Bradford looking for somewhere to stay. I hated the police and I never failed to let them know it. They took Paul and me back home to our respective families. My mother made a show of how happy she was that I was safe, but I knew I was in for it after the police had gone. It was just like so many occasions before: while the law was around everyone in the family acted pleasantly; concerned, relieved that the young ruffian was home at last. When they left things would turn nasty and I would get a beating.

My crimes continued and as I got older I was regularly hauled into court. My family would make a big deal about it and my mother usually came with me, but I wasn't afraid of being there. I genuinely didn't care. At my first court appearance I got a twelve month supervision order for four counts of criminal damage. Consequently, I ended up having a social worker assigned to me whom I had to see regularly as part of the order. I can't remember much about him or our chats together other than it was a drag and whatever was said went in one ear and out the other.

At this point in my life I lived to hang out in gangs and our main occupation had become drinking bottles of cider laced with Anadin, Paracetamol, sleeping pills or anything that the gang members could get their hands on. As often as I could I would retreat with a bag of glue to a derelict building, sometimes with others, sometimes by myself, and sniff the fumes to bring on a hallucinatory high. It was the most powerful kick I'd had to date and sometimes I lost total control and became unconscious. On occasion I would come round and discover the now dry bag still clutched in my hand with bite marks on it like I had tried to eat it. I had some weird hallucinations, but none that I can really remember. It was also around this time that a friend from down the street showed me his dad's huge stash of pornography hidden in the garden shed. I became fascinated with the magazines straight away and often tried to sneak into the shed to look at them, even without my friend being there. It was yet another pull into a seedy sub-culture where I would exist for a long time to come.

At some point I belonged to a gang which had a skull emblem smeared in blood on their jackets. I felt like I had come of age. Perhaps that had happened a long time before, I don't know. I was a young boy, robbed of his innocence long ago through the shock of dysfunctional relationships and abuse. It had turned me into someone other than who God intended me to be. My street cred was growing and I fancied myself as a hard man, just like Streetfighter Billy. Carrying a knife became routine for me. I never went anywhere without one and I often wondered what it would feel like to stab my stepfather. Thoughts of committing violence nagged my mind and Allan was the top of my list of recipients. I wondered how long it might be until my thoughts would become a reality.

Chapter 2

I was developing into a total rebel and at that stage of my teens I felt invincible. I dressed like a skinhead and my behaviour was always very loud, foul mouthed and abusive. Even though I had hardly seen much of him due to his many spells in prison and his separation from my mother, I wanted to be like my dad. In fact, I saw him very rarely after he and Mum split up, but those few occasions made a deep impression on me. His reputation preceded him. I loved the notoriety associated to the mere mention of his name. I liked his hard macho exterior, the way he smelt of booze and the fact that people didn't mess with him.

Each time I saw Dad I felt so excited. Once he turned up at our house completely out of the blue when my stepfather Allan was at home. I watched in sheer fascination as Allan squirmed self-consciously. I could tell he was really scared of Dad. He had heard of my father's reputation for violence and was uncharacteristically smiley and polite. Sitting on the sofa next to my dad, I couldn't help wondering what would happen if I told him how much my brother and I got beaten by the man sitting awkwardly across the room. After the visit my dad went off to see some of his old friends on the estate who he used to go rabbiting with, and I went with him. It felt great to be associated with this feared and revered man. Another time I was in bed when Dad visited the house. On this occasion Mum and Allan were out at the pub and as usual Danny was babysitting. When Dad left Danny rushed up to the bedroom to wake me up and showed me what he had left behind – a sub-machine gun. Fascinated with war and weapons as I was, I thought it was the coolest thing I'd ever seen in my life.

Although Mum didn't get on with Dad's mum, Eileen Rowan, she did let me go and stay with her occasionally. I loved my gran so much. To me she was the equivalent of Marlon Brando in the *Godfather* movies. She would say it how it was – no messing! She always referred to my mother as "Flossy Light Food" which I found quite funny, though I had no idea what it meant. One weekend while I was there Dad turned up. Gran immediately laid into him for turning up smelling of booze. She really let him have it. Dad didn't take anything from anyone and I found it really strange that from Gran he just took it on the chin and said nothing.

Dad asked Gran if he could take me rabbiting with him the next morning. Knowing that I hardly ever saw him and it was too good an opportunity to miss, she said yes. So off I went with my father to his house to stay over, ready for the next morning's excursion. We set off walking across the fields. My dad walked everywhere. If he could, he would always take a shortcut through the fields. He loved the countryside and was never happier than when he was outdoors with his dogs, shooting and "living off the land". He was in his element. When we reached his place he packed me off to bed early because we were going to be up at five the next morning. But before he did we had a play fight. It was a good natured brawl. He could have swatted me like a fly if he'd wanted to.

At dawn next morning we were sitting having breakfast when Dad's friend who was coming with us arrived. We fetched the dogs and set off, the men carrying the nets and me the ferrets. Dad had a huge knife slung in his belt. The dogs weren't pets, they were workers and well trained. As soon as they saw a rabbit they were off after it, with us running behind them. When the rabbit disappeared down a hole we would put the ferret down and wait for it to bolt. Immediately the rabbit was caught Dad would gut it with his knife there and then and let the ferrets eat the innards and taste the blood. My job was to wait by the hole and try to coax the blood-hungry ferret towards me as it emerged from the hole. All was going fine until I saw Dad lurch towards me and boot what I thought was the ferret into the air. I discovered that it was actually a large rat running towards me! That experience took the shine of my rabbiting experience somewhat, but it was still a great day. I cherished these experiences with my father.

Back home at Windybank life went on as normal with me regularly getting myself into trouble. My parents' already thin patience with me was wearing ever thinner. It was ready to snap altogether when one day Allan left his window cleaner's belt hanging over the banisters with his day's wages in it. Without a moment's hesitation I stole all the money from his belt and ran away. As usual I headed towards the fields. The countryside was always my first port of call. Perhaps it was because it allowed me a sense of freedom; it let me feel like my dad for a while, going wherever he wanted, answerable to no one but himself. More likely it was just a relief to get out of our claustrophobic little house and breath some fresh air, away from the suffocating presence of my stepfather and surrogate brothers. On this occasion, for some reason, I thought that if I followed the direction of the wires of the electricity pylons through the fields they would eventually lead me to the beach. I hadn't been going long when the police managed to locate and apprehend me once again. Yet again I was delivered back home and once again it was all smiles in front of the police officers. Later Allan beat me relentlessly and sent me to bed. Oddly enough, the beatings didn't hurt any more. I was used to it.

Sometimes a little gang of us would take a walk up to a nearby motorway service station that was accessible from the fields. Inside the services there was a little amusement arcade and when no one was looking we would stuff toilet paper up inside the one-armed bandit machines above the metal tray where the money is supposed to come out. We would hang around and watch from a distance for ages while various people came and played on the machines. When they had a win and no money came out, naturally they would go and complain. While they were away we would run over, pull out the toilet paper and grab the money. In the course of an evening we could repeat this process two or three times collecting a fair bit of money and spending it on whatever we wanted. Another of our amusement arcade scams was to wrap some very thin wire around a ten pence piece which would then be dropped into the money slot of a machine. By holding on to it very carefully you could actually manoeuvre it back out and then drop it in again. By repeating the process over and over you could clock up the amount of credit you wanted on a particular machine, then pull the coin back out and play. Service stations were good places to go hunting for pornography. We found that lorry drivers routinely dumped magazines they'd read in the litter bins dotted around the car park, not wanting to leave them in their trucks or take them home where their wives might find them. We would rummage through the bins, collect as many as possible and then go down the fields to read them, which fuelled our interest in girls all the more.

Another of our favourite haunts was a racetrack and stadium, with a gym and bar area, a few miles away from our estate. In broad daylight we used to climb in through the changing-room windows and, while people were in the shower or running on the track, go through their coats and trousers and take their wallets and car keys. Since none of us could drive and we didn't know what to do with their credit cards, we used to throw these away and just keep the money. I was very aware that because of my age I couldn't go to prison and that, if I got caught, I would probably only get a good kicking, which was a price I was prepared to pay.

Stealing gave me a huge buzz. Around this time I also began breaking into houses and factories, looking for money. I enjoyed the reputation I was building for myself of being fearless. I would brag about the jobs I had done and later started taking people with me to show off how good I was. It was all the better for me if they got really scared while we were turning over someone's house – then I could really tease them about it afterwards.

In 1984 I was arrested for the umpteenth time and charged with two counts of burglary, with six further charges to be taken into consideration. I was sentenced to thirty-six hours' attendance at Dewsbury Young Offenders Institution. My time would be spread out over a number of Saturdays. Since it was about five miles away from home it meant that someone had to take me there every weekend. Needless to say this did not go down well at home. Mum and Allan were at the end of their tether over me. There were interminable arguments about what to do with me, during which my stepfather usually threatened, "Either he goes, or I go." Usually these rows took place with me standing by listening. Mum was pregnant again at the time and it wound me up terribly to hear myself constantly being denigrated in front of my seven brothers – soon to be eight. I didn't want to be humiliated in front of them. But the threat of embarrassment certainly wasn't enough to control my behaviour. Whilst I was still doing my stint at Dewsbury I stole a week's rent money from home and ran off to spend the lot at a local fairground.

Dewsbury was meant to be a short, sharp shock, I think. For me it was just another experience and I took it in my stride. It was actually something else to brag about, like the present-day Anti-Social Behaviour Orders that are handed out to unruly teenagers. Many see them as a badge of honour, not a deterrent that will persuade them to change their ways. All the lads at Dewsbury were about the same age as I was and it was run like an army training camp. We had to call the people in charge "Sir" and march, stand to attention and all that kind of stuff. There was lots of physical activity like press-ups, running and jumping over a wooden horse. It was nothing I couldn't handle easily. Needless to say, it didn't "work" if its aim was to pull me into line and alter my behaviour. My memory of events around that time is a little hazy, but I think that before I'd even finished the last of my sessions there I was hauled back into court charged with theft and attempted burglary. The courts didn't like me and I didn't like them.

Allan was serious about his ultimatum. My mum made her choice and it wasn't me. She was there in court the day I was taken into care and so was my Auntie Cheryl whom I have always loved very much. The words of the team of people who were busy deciding my future went completely over my head. All I could hear were my stepfather's words going round and round in my mind: "Either he goes, or I go." I would have loved the judge to rule that I could go and live with my grandmother, but he didn't. I was placed in care. My mother went in one direction and I went in another. At that moment something happened inside me: in my heart I vowed that when I was old enough I would go back and take revenge on my stepfather. I couldn't understand how my mother could possibly choose to stay with a man who shouted at her all the time and beat her at the drop of a hat. It totally floored me.

I arrived at Rivendell Children's Home in Dewsbury feeling utterly rejected by my family. My stay there would not last too long, but I didn't know that at the time. To me it was a hollow depressing, environment; we were a collection of abandoned, unruly young people looking for some kind of security and meaning. But as well as being depressing it was dangerous and destructive. Some of the lads there were heavily into alcohol and glue sniffing. One boy, I remember, used to self-harm and he would show the staff the raw, deep gashes he'd made on his wrists.

Away from home for the first time I felt quite crazy. There was always a simmering, underlying tension amongst the inhabitants and trouble was likely to erupt at a moment's notice. One day I got into a fight with one of the other lads and I went completely over the top, freaking out. I wanted to smash his head in. When a member of staff tried to stop me, I then turned on him. Eventually, after a fierce struggle, several staff members working together managed to lock me in a room. I guess they thought I would calm down eventually and then they could talk to me, reason with me. Instead, empowered by my anger and the boiling frustration of being prevented from fighting back during so many beatings, I managed to heave a wardrobe through the nearest window. I climbed out of the window, jumped down, ran around to the front of the house, burst through the front door, leapt on the lad I'd been brawling with and continued the fight!

A few weeks later three of us stole a member of staff's car keys from her handbag and went joy-riding in her car. This was a new kind of thrill I'd not experienced before and it gave me a huge adrenalin rush. Coming round a corner at high speed we nearly killed ourselves smashing into some metal railings. We could so easily have been wiped out, but to us it was a great laugh. Never mind the damage and all the strife we were causing, we were letting off steam and we would do anything to break up our humdrum days. The incident put me back in court again. This time I received a conditional discharge for two years. Rivendell had had enough of me after this and shortly after I was moved to another home in Castle Howard in north Yorkshire.

Castle Howard was a good fifty plus miles north east of my home town and in the middle of nowhere. It was the furthest away from home I had ever been and although it's drivable in an hour, it seemed much further to me. The distance just added to my feelings of separation from my family. As far as I was concerned, I was on my own now and I would do what I needed to do to survive. The home at Castle Howard comprised a massive complex with three housing blocks, teaching accommodation, a secure unit, a chapel, a gym, a farm and a football field, all grouped around a green paddock. The girls lived in what they called "1 House" and the boys in "2 House" and "3 House". Most of the kids were from the

Scunthorpe/Grimsby/Hull area and were on remand for crimes they had committed. We were all around the same age.

Like Dewsbury, there was always a lot of gym work at Castle Howard. I think they thought that if we expended a lot of physical energy we would be less likely to kick off, so they kept us busy the whole time. On my first day there we were taken to the gym to play indoor football. It was very fast and violent with everyone trying to prove something. Whenever I had the chance I went in quite hard on one of the members of staff called Mr Tate who I'd discovered used to play football for Leeds. At one point he came up on me from behind and shouldered me. I went flying, really cracking my head on the wall. Everyone seemed to stop to see what the new boy would do, but I just laughed and said, "Your walls down 'ere are harder than ours back home." He laughed and we became good friends. There were two other Tates on the staff – Mr and Mrs Tate. I'm not sure how they were all related, but I became very friendly with all of them.

Because most of the other kids at Castle Howard were on remand, whereas I was on a care order, as the months passed by all the faces in the place would change except mine. One thing that really bugged me was that everyone else would get mail from their family on a regular basis – especially when birthdays and Christmas came around. I never received a thing and I made no secret of the fact that I hated my family. I channelled my anger by becoming obsessed with fitness and weight training. I spent every possible moment pounding the gym's punch bag, running round the field, or pumping weights in the weight room. I think Mr Tate saw the aggression in me and understood the effect my home situation was having on me. He got me a benching chest bar so I could still work out when I couldn't go to the gym. At mealtimes he would also hold back all the leftover vegetables and fruit for me and would egg me on to eat more. "Come on, you can eat more than that!" he would say. He also got me to join the football team, knowing full well what would happen. I was always put in defence. Any player, no matter how big or how small, who came near me with the ball would get brought to the ground with a massive scissor chop.

We played quite a lot of five-a-side football, but I always looked forward to the end of the game when we would play "murder ball". One group of lads would be at one end of the hall and another group at the other end. A heavy medicine ball was placed in the middle of the hall and when the whistle was blown, both teams would charge towards the ball and try to get it to the opposite team's end. If it can be compared to anything I suppose it was loosely like rugby or American Football, but with no rules. In murder ball anything goes and you can use any tactic to win. Someone always got hurt, but then that was the whole point. We loved it.

Although there were classrooms at Castle Howard I don't remember ever having any teaching there. I only remember a classroom where we used to do a bit of woodwork or metalwork and mess around with the soldering irons. The staff did put us to work on the small farm, however, mucking out the animals and feeding the pigs. Though we were supposed to be working, usually when I was working outside, I, and whoever was with me at the time, would sneak off down to where the Land Rovers were parked, tie a rag onto a broom handle and stick it down into the petrol tank until it was soaked. After we had "prepared" a couple of rags we would stuff them into a carrier bag, find somewhere to hide and then sniff them, hallucinating until all the fumes had evaporated. Considering the number of times I did this it makes me wonder how I am still alive today. I'm still here by the grace of God alone. We would even smoke cigarettes immediately after inhaling petrol fumes. I only ever got caught doing it once. After that the staff were more vigilant and I had to find new ways of getting high. But I was incorrigibly resourceful and my imagination was an endless source of invention. I found that another way of getting a buzz was by drying out a banana skin on my radiator and then smoking it. Whenever I experienced these highs I would do all sorts of mad things like running at walls and doing somersaults off them or jumping from crazy heights.

I became part of the furniture at Castle Howard. As time went on I was even allowed little privileges like being allowed to go over to see the girls in 1 House when no one else was, which was cool. But even with such occasional perks in the end I was sick and tired of being stuck there and I decided I was going to run away and have some fun. The first time another boy and I escaped over the fence and ran into the surrounding woods. Feeling free again for the first time in ages we explored deep into the woods until we found a railway line which we followed for miles and miles. Along the way we kept stopping to pick wild garlic leaves. We planned to dry them out later so that we could make joints and smoke them. Our freedom was fairly short-lived as we were caught about five miles away in Malton that same day.

The second time I ran away it was much further. This time I and another lad, Steve, managed abscond fifty miles south east of Castle Howard and get as far as Hull on the coast. We got there by train. Compared to the little towns I was used to Hull seemed massive. As far as I was concerned it was the big city! Our chosen destination was Hull because Steve had some good mates there. As soon as we arrived we hooked up with them, found a flat we could break into and gathered there for a glue sniffing session. Someone must have seen us going in, however, because a little while later the police showed up. In a panic we vacated the flat, scattered and all ran in separate directions with the police in hot pursuit. I managed to get away without being caught. My problem was, I was on the run in a big city and I had no idea where I was running. The fact that I was in a semi-hallucinatory state didn't help matters. I ended up wandering around the city for hours until my head cleared and I stumbled across the city centre's main bus station. I recognised this place because once previously, as a concession for never going home, I had been allowed to travel on the minibus which dropped the kids who were going home for the weekend off at various stops in Hull, Grimsby and Scunthorpe. With no money to my name and nowhere to go I admitted defeat. I sat at the bus station for a very long time until the Castle Howard minibus came. It was lucky for me that I had run away on a Sunday. Sunday was picking-up day. The driver, who was a member of staff, never said a word to me – not as I got on the bus nor all the way back to Castle Howard. He just kept looking at me in his mirror and smiling to himself. Even though I'd run away I wasn't punished for it. It was as if the staff understood I had nothing to lose.

I had been at Castle Howard a few months when the staff decided to introduce swimming as a new activity in their weekly programme. I thought this was great because it meant a trip out to the nearby city of York. After we had been regulars there for a few weeks, we were swimming one day when we noticed some girls banging on the windows. They were standing outside on the grass watching us through the floor-to-ceiling glass and giggling to each other. Communicating through the glass I managed to give them Castle Howard's phone number and my name and they started calling us. After a few phone calls I decided to run away to York to meet up with them. Each week we were given around £2 spending money. I saved mine so that I could catch the bus to York. I ran and hid in the cornfield behind the bus stop, hoping the bus would come before the pre-dinner roll call took place, during which I would be conspicuously absent. Fortunately for me, it did. Seeing the bus coming down the road I hurried out of my hiding place, jumped on the bus, and kept myself well hidden in the corner on the back seat.

Once in York I found my way to one of the girls' houses and she called her friends to come round. There was a generous supply of alcohol in the house and soon we were all drinking. Typically, since I did everything to excess, by the end of the evening I was drunk and puking up everywhere. The girl thought it would be a good idea to put up a tent for me in the back garden to hide me from her father who was a taxi driver in York and who was out working all evening. In theory, I could sleep it off here without being discovered or disturbed. Unfortunately I was woken up in the early hours of the morning by someone trying to get into the tent. I shouted and pulled my knife out on the very shocked intruder – the girl's father, no doubt wondering why a tent had been put up in his back garden. The feeble explanation that I was his daughter's friend who was staying over for the night did nothing to calm him down. He made his daughter tell him where I was from and drove me back to Castle Howard immediately. When I knocked on the door the staff just let me in as if nothing had happened. I wasn't punished in any way – not even a telling off. If any of the other kids had done the same they would have been in "big trouble". I couldn't understand why they just let me get away with it, other than they felt sorry for me.

It was at Castle Howard that I got my first tattoo. I thought tattoos were cool – still do – and I really wanted one. I wanted to stand out. At the time I only knew one or two people of my age who had them. It sounds stupid now but I was making a statement. Precisely what that statement was I'm not entirely sure, but it marked me out as an individual and I liked that. I wasn't part of the establishment. I was a rebel. A guy from Hull did the tattoo. We stole some Indian ink from the office and managed to get hold of a needle and cotton. We wrapped the cotton around the bottom of the needle and we were off. On my right hand he tattooed "Mark", one letter for each finger. The theory behind this was that every time I punched someone in the face they would know who the punch was from. Later that day, when no one was around, I went upstairs where there was a big mirror and did a tattoo on my face. I had met people with a single dot tattooed under their left eye. When I asked what it stood for they had told me it was something you got when you went to borstal. The people I knew who had these dots were all criminals. So I tattooed a black dot under my left eye because I identified with them. I was a criminal too and I actually wanted people to know it. In crime I had found something I was good at.

At the end of my second year at Castle Howard there was a review of my care order. My mother and my social worker came to the meeting at which a date was agreed for me to go back home. When I eventually did return home it was an absolute disaster. The family had moved to a district called Laverhills, a ten-minute walk from the Windybank estate where we used to live. The new house was three times the size of the old one. My brothers and stepfather were all smiles and were being very nice to me when I arrived. I was shown to what would be my room. Despite their attempts at welcoming me, it all felt very false indeed. I didn't believe for a minute that they actually wanted me back there. My stepbrother Danny, the eldest of Allan's sons, had moved into a high-rise flat in Brooklyn Flats, an area full of drugs and wild parties. For a short time everything seemed to be going OK. Since I had no access to a gym I got hold of a pole which I put through some house bricks and began weight-lifting in my bedroom. Things had changed at home in that now it was my brother Wayne who was always being shouted at, punished and banished to his room. Having become much stronger than I used to be through relentless weight training, gym work and running I realized that Allan didn't frighten me any more. He didn't seem the imposing, threatening figure that I remembered. At weekends, after closing time at the pub, he would invite lots of people back to drink at the house. On one occasion I was up getting a drink when I saw a sailor trying to kiss my friend's mum. So, there and then in our crowded front room, I gave him a right hook, knocking him out cold on the carpet. Everyone was stunned. My mother started shouting and screaming, but I stormed off in victory. I wanted to fight the world.

After this I had another spell in care, this time at a place called Eastmore. I don't remember too much about it because I was only there for a very short while. After my stint there the authorities decided I could try living at home again. Despite the new house and, as they perhaps thought of it, the new start my mum and stepfather had made, when I returned home from care again I found myself confronted by the same old scenario I had lived with daily a couple of years before. One day I was in my bedroom chatting to my brothers when we heard Mum and Allan rowing downstairs. There was an audible smack followed by a scream and we knew that Allan was laying into her. In years gone by all of us, me included, would have hung our heads and done nothing; hating the fact that our mum was being physically abused but powerless to do anything to stop it. Now things were different. I leaped off my bed and charged downstairs. I flung open the living room door and saw Allan standing there over my mum. Without hesitation I punched him in the mouth as hard as I could sending him flying backwards. He hit the nearest wall, slid down it and landed on his backside. I was far from finished with him and as I was giving it to him my stepbrother Alan junior ran downstairs and started shouting at me to stop. I turned on him next and began punching him as well. I had completely lost it. It was then that my mother began screaming at me to get out of the house. I couldn't understand it: I thought she would be happy that I was protecting her. I was deeply hurt and confused. Did my mum *want* to be abused by this bully? My emotions swirled with the realisation that, at the same time, I was elated by the feeling of seeing Allan hit the floor. The adrenalin rush was amazing. I had had my revenge and I was prepared to give him some more when the next opportunity came up.

Chapter 3

Since I wasn't exactly welcome at home I moved in with my gran for a while. She was a practical, down-to-earth person who made sure you got something to eat and that you took plenty of exercise. She had never liked my mother much and neither did I at that point. While I was living with her I got to know a girl who lived locally. We started going out together and very soon she announced that she was pregnant. When she also told me, however, that the baby wasn't mine I flipped and had a fight with the bloke she claimed was the father. By now I was eighteen years old and burgling continuously. I had two partners in crime who I worked with regularly – brothers named Andy and Nick who lived in the same street as my family.

I couldn't live with my gran long term and I knew I had to find somewhere else to live pretty quickly. Through Andy and Nick I was put in touch with a woman called Sue who was looking for a lodger. She was living on her own and had two kids so she needed some extra income. She lived directly opposite the brothers which of course proved highly convenient for us and our "business". What was very strange for me was living so close, just a stone's throw away, from my family. My mother lived just a few doors down and yet we never, ever spoke. The hatred was mutual.

From my new location I could easily pop across the street and hang out with the brothers. Andy and Nick were almost as crazy as me. Their house was decorated in the weirdest of colours and Andy had a baby doll hanging by the window in his bedroom with a knife in its head. We all loved loud music and whenever we were at home it would be blaring out, deafening half the street. We were almost always on the look-out to rob. On an evening we would be out stealing motorbikes in order to go and pull a job somewhere or just for a joyride and then we would dump them afterwards. Mainly we burgled factories. I remember at one job Nick deliberately cut his hands on the broken glass of a window and in big letters all down the corridor wrote the words "kill" and "bastards" in blood. Then we rampaged through the whole building smashing doors looking for the keys to the safe. Adrenalin pumping we stood in front of the three-foot-high safe trying all the keys we had found and then we made off with the contents of the safe and all the computers. Nick lost a lot of blood but it was good fun. We had a real laugh when the next day we read in the local paper that, because of the blood, the factory owners thought the burglary was something to do with witchcraft.

During the daytime the three of us would spend time just hanging out together smoking weed, joint after joint. In order to "score" some drugs I would travel to Manningham Lane in Bradford, which at the time was in the heart of the red light district. It was an area buzzing with the dubious "life" of the sex and drugs subculture. On a typical evening there would be prostitutes clamouring for business, desperate to generate some custom in order to buy themselves a fix; music pounding from cars; and drug dealers arguing amongst themselves over who had seen you first, claiming you as "their" customer. On one occasion after I had scored I was arrested. I tried to throw the stuff away as the police hauled me in for questioning, but they saw me do it and I ended up being charged with possession of controlled drugs.

Spending all my time at Andy and Nick's house I got to know their sister Mandy and we formed a relationship of sorts. It wasn't long until she was pregnant with my child, but I hardly spent any time with her. Sometimes she would come across to Sue's house and sleep there with me. She must have found it strange that every now and then I would sleep with a rifle under the mattress. Just like my dad I would often get up very early, go out by myself into the countryside and shoot anything that resembled a rabbit. I didn't have the same motivation as my dad though. I wasn't trying to live off the land; I did it for no other reason than the pleasure of killing something. I did love Mandy, but on the nights when she was not there I would end up having sex with Sue. I saw it as paying my rent – that was how my mind worked. On other nights I would go and sleep at Mandy's house so that her brother Nick could go and sleep with Sue.

After a while I began to get fussy about who I would go burgling with. I was no longer satisfied with a three-way split, so just two of us went instead. We would usually smoke dope and watch videos till around two in the morning, giving everyone a chance to get to bed, and then we would set off. It was an unspoken rule that we never came home empty handed. Often we had no transport so we would carry the stuff we stole, usually computers and fax machines, over fields and railways – sometimes for miles – stopping every ten minutes to give our arms a rest. As the sun was beginning to rise we would hide our stuff in a field, camouflaging it with bushes and leaves, and come back later in the day with a potential buyer in tow. We could always find people who wanted to buy the stuff we stole and usually they would mention certain things they were after so that we basically then stole to order. If the computers were quite new, we would strip out the serial numbers and give them new ones before selling them through some of our friends' shops. We would always spend the money on clothes or drugs. In one day we could easily blow £400 each on drugs.

At some stage the police caught up with the three of us and we were all charged. In my case, as I recall, for two burglaries and stealing a motorbike. Both Andy and Nick had already been to prison. Up until then I hadn't, but that was about to change. When we arrived at the magistrate's court and had our hearing, all three of us stood side by side – me with a stupid grin all over my face – as the judge read out the charges. First he remanded Andy and then Nick into custody and, last of all, as they were being led down, he granted me bail. I couldn't understand why I was being treated differently and went berserk. Any normal person, I know, would have been relieved to be off the hook. I wasn't. I began shouting abuse and demanding that I should go to prison with my pals. I can still remember the look on the face of my solicitor who had put up a brave fight for my bail and got it for me. The judge couldn't understand it either. But my carefully chosen words had the desired effect and I too was remanded into custody. Of course, everyone thought I was mad! But that was my mentality at that time – I saw it as being loyal to my friends. I was going to stand by them no matter what.

And so I was taken into custody, but my first ever experience of prison wasn't at all what I was expecting. After waiting in a holding cell for about five hours we were all handcuffed, bundled into the back of a van and driven to HMP Armley on the outskirts of Leeds. All the way there, as the van went from place to place picking up prisoners from other courts, we just laughed and joked. Not long after we had left Leeds, Nick said, "There it is!" On the hill ahead of us stood a huge black castle with massive gates covered in bars and razor wire. As we got closer I wondered what I had let myself in for. Not that it mattered really. The prison gates opened and officers with snarling, barking dogs pointed the way in. We were taken in, un-cuffed and directed into a small room with about twenty people, all of whom were smoking and generally talking about what had happened at court, what sentence they had received, who'd got drugs for the night, who was waiting to smash whose head in, etc., etc. This was the kind of conversation I was comfortable with. The men's crimes ranged from murder to burglary to wounding someone with a machete.

After some time we were called out one by one and had to give our name. We were then given a number and moved to another room which had more people packed in like cattle, some actually smoking joints. Everyone was talking or shouting. After another three hours we were individually called to a room where each of us was strip searched. I was told to take all my clothes off, stand on a platform, turn around and squat down. After being searched for drugs I was told to stand up again, my clothes were taken from me and I was handed a towel. The prison officers told me to follow the yellow line on the floor which led round the corner until I came eventually to a shower. After showering I was given prison-issue clothes – a very creased green shirt with a massive collar, a pair of grubby-looking brown jeans and a pair of shoes which stank. For underwear you either got boxer shorts or massive Y-fronts. Most people's stuff was either too big or too small. If you wanted good kit you had to pay the lads dishing it out for it, either with tobacco or drugs – that was their perk. Their mates got sorted for free. All the young prisoners under twenty-one, which seemed to be most of us, were wearing green. The cons over twenty-one had a different-coloured shirt. Eventually we were all given our bed rolls to carry to our cells up on the landings.

What hit me first was the stink of urine and the filth of the language of the lads shouting out of the window of their cells to one another. In each wing there were three landings with about thirty cells on each floor. I was given a card with a number on; I waited for Andy and Nick to get theirs so I could see where they were. We laughed as we said goodbye to each other and then I went off to find my cell. Before going in I checked the card outside the door to see the name of the person I was sharing with and what sentence he was serving; then I looked through the spy hole before finally going in. It didn't really matter who it was: I had no choice anyway. An officer unlocked the cell and ushered me in. All there was in the tiny, stinking cell was a double bunk, a table, a chair, a locker and a very smelly bucket in the corner surrounded by cigarette butts. But what struck me most was the pornography. It was plastered everywhere – on the ceiling, on the walls, inside the locker. This, I was to discover, was normal. In the spaces where there were no pictures, people had written what sentences they were serving and where they were from. There were stains on the walls where people had thrown trays of food against the wall in anger and other dubious marks where they had obviously been picking their nose. On the back wall there were two very small, arch-shaped windows, covered by bars which were just wide-enough apart to get your hand through.

I introduced myself to my cell mate and we asked each other the usual questions: what are you in for? how long for? where are you from? We both weighed each other up. Since it was obvious anyway, I told him I was a first-timer and then bombarded him with an avalanche of questions. As we were chatting I heard someone bang on the ceiling of our cell and then shout "Mark". It was Nick. I went to the tiny window and shouted back. There, dangling down right in front of me was a piece of string with a roll-up on it. Laughing, I reached through the bars to get it. This was my first line. Let me explain: in prison if you need to get anything to anybody, you tear tiny strands off the end of the green blanket on your bed, tie them together, and then tie a weight onto it along with whatever you want to pass down on the end of it. You swing it out of the window and it gets passed from cell to cell until it reaches the person you want to get it to – all the while watching carefully via a tiny mirror held outside the cell window to make sure no one pulls it into their cell and pinches what's on it before your mate reels the goodies in. Being in a cell twenty-three hours a day means the "line" is your lifeline. Nick and I chatted out of the window for a while and then got our heads down.

The next morning was an eye-opener. The cell door was unlocked. I stepped out of the door to find about fifty men queuing up with buckets full of pee and turds. Man, it stank! There were wet patches all over the floor where the slop had been spilt. I joined the queue. I spotted one or two people I knew and gave them a loud shout. Everyone was shouting, trying to do a quick deal while the doors were open. I could see enormous cockroaches floating in the urine and some more squashed on the floor. Below me I could see the cages of wire mesh extending across to the other landings. I knew it was there to stop anyone thrown over the rail hitting the ground below. I asked if it had ever happened and was told it had. I could see a prison guard standing just below me and was very tempted to throw my entire bucket over him. Apparently it had happened many times before. I would have loved to see it! After slop-out the officers shouted, "Slop-out's finished. Get in your f****** cells, you b*******." I hated the screws (officers) – really hated them. Some of them told me they knew my father and that he was one of their regulars. I often got cheeky and told them where to go. The "breakfast" that followed the slop-out was awful.

You got one hour of exercise a day, but if it rained you didn't get any and that was that. If you did something wrong you had to submit to what was known as "Part 1 of 27", which meant that you had to stand by the door, stick your chin out and take a slap from the prison officer who unlocked the door. The whole landing exercised at the same time so you got a chance to chat to your mates. You all walked round and round in a big circle. If it was a sunny day people would generally sit on the grass for the whole hour. This was the time of day to do anything you needed to do: buy or sell drugs, get some tobacco, smash someone's head in. I saw numerous fights. Everyone seemed to belong to a gang or clique, depending on where you came from. The inmates were mostly Scousers, Mancunians and Yorkies because of the proximity of the prison to those regions. If someone from Bradford started a fight and you were from near Bradford, you were for the Bradford guy. Sometimes a fight would break out between one whole region and another. In other words, if you started a fight with one Yorkie, you had to fight them all. That was how most people survived. There were a few people who had sufficient reputations on the outside that they were left well alone inside. No one messed with them. Typically it was the weak ones who were singled out, bullied and threatened, and their wages demanded from them leaving them nothing. In fear and desperation some of them went to the officers and asked to be put on a protection wing for their own safety.

One evening a week we were taken to the chapel in the prison to watch a video. More often than not it was some kind of thriller and the sound was always very loud. On one occasion there was a guy sitting in front of me with a big bushy beard. While he was trying to watch the film, the man next to him kept teasing him. This continued for a while but nothing happened. Clearly not getting the response he wanted, the second guy whipped out a lighter from nowhere and set fire to the first guy's beard. A fight broke out and almost a riot as everyone kicked off.

Anyone suspected of being a grass (an informant) inside was in big trouble. They were always targeted and word would get around quickly whenever something was going down. At an opportune moment, usually during exercise time, the grass would be surrounded, casually yet slickly as a number of people crowded around him, and then "bang", someone would whack him, usually with a wooden leg pulled off their cell table, and as many people as possible would put the boot in before the screws arrived to break it up. The man on the floor usually got spat on before everyone casually walked on. If it was a one-on-one grudge fight then all the other inmates would form a large, tight circle around the fighters which would hinder the screws' efforts to get in and stop the fight, prolonging the proceedings for as long as possible. Everyone loved a fight and would be cheering and shouting, hungry for blood to be drawn, happy for the entertainment. With riot bells ringing and whistles blowing, the officers would come from every direction, as many as twenty at a time accompanied by snarling dogs. Everyone cheered while the two fighters were dragged back to the block.

Being in a cell for twenty-three hours a day you begin to feel like a caged animal, so you start to act like one. There was always an atmosphere of tension and you sensed that the balance between relative peace and sudden violence balanced on a knife edge. Anything could happen at any time. But when things were quiet and nothing was kicking off we tended to talk a lot. In prison there's not a lot else to do. You talk with each other about the crimes you've committed and discuss how you did them. As you can imagine, you hear numerous new ways of doing things that you hadn't thought of before and you make a lot of contacts in the criminal underworld. Each time you go back to court and are put on remand again you tend to get assigned to a different cell with a different cell mate. It doesn't matter whether or not you get on, you're all in the same boat. In prison you meet a lot of angry, violent and rebellious people.

One of my cell mates taught me how to protect myself if ever I was on the receiving end of a mob attack and how to make a weapon to do some damage to someone quickly and get maximum effect. The first way is to use the leg off your cell table hidden in your jacket. I've seen blokes knocked out by one and it isn't pretty. The second way is to put batteries in a sock. The third and best way is to modify the razor issued to every prisoner to shave with as these are always left in the cell. You smash the plastic holder, take out the razor blade and melt it into the end of a toothbrush to make a makeshift knife. Some people would melt two blades into the end of the toothbrush with a matchstick in between to hold them apart, so the victim would be cut twice. The twisted thinking behind this was that it was only possible to stitch up one of the wounds, so you knew you were going to scar the person for life. You would find blades taken out of their razor in every cell – most people used them to split matches into two to make them last longer.

There were many nights when, lying in your bed, you would hear someone screaming and smashing up their cell. They had lost it, gone over the edge. Then everyone, including me, would stand by the window of their cell and start shouting, "Go on mate, smash it up and then hang yourself. You can do it." It was entertainment. There was no respect. Gradually everyone would get more and more wound up and then someone would set fire to their sheet or blanket and push it through the tiny cell window to try and burn the place down. Men from other cells would pile their sheets on top. When the screws finally came to put the fire out the inmates would heap abuse on them and rattle their plastic cups between the bars, trying to spit on them without being seen. The atmosphere was electric and the noise was deafening with men shouting and banging on their doors and kicking them. When the fire had been put out and the bloke who had started smashing up his cell in the first place had been busted, everything would go back to normal: there would be lines of drugs being snorted everywhere, people passing matches or tobacco or selling cannabis. The score was half an ounce of tobacco for a single joint, which was a lot of money in prison terms. As the allowance at that time was about £2 per week, you could just about afford half an ounce. I myself made dozens of such deals. When it all went quiet again, most people had a small radio to stop them going mad, but occasionally the sound of someone singing would drift down the corridor.

Sometimes you would hear people encouraging their cell mate to "slash themselves up", which is what we used to call cutting your wrists. People wanted others to harm themselves, purely for selfish reasons. You could make a plea for bail in court on the grounds of the stress of waking up with a dead body in your cell. And it worked sometimes. It was a dog-eat-dog world. Suicide attempts were quite common. As well as slashing their wrists, people would try and hang themselves by tying their bed sheet to the bars of the window when their cell mate was asleep, leaving a suicide note for their loved ones. Not everyone made it to their death, but some did.

Amid this bleak and depressing cycle people always looked forward to their weekly visit to court for their remand to be renewed. It was a day out. I would always be cheeky to the magistrates because it was still all just a game to me. I was not quite so sure of myself when, after months of waiting, our big day in the Crown Court came up. I was convinced I was going to get sent down for years. For once the atmosphere in the prison van was subdued. Everyone had waited a long time for this day and was anxious about what the outcome would be. We were taken first to the holding cell where other prisoners were already waiting. It was dark and dismal with bars floor to ceiling. People had brought cannabis to calm their nerves and the joints were passed around. When each man's case came up he was taken up the stairs handcuffed to two officers, re-appearing either grim-faced or jubilant when he had been sentenced: seven years, three years, twelve months depending on whether it was armed robbery, burglary, grievous bodily harm or shoplifting. Finally we were up. To my surprise I was given the maximum hours of community service which I knew would include the usual mundane gardening and decorating duties. Andy and Nick, who both had more previous convictions than I had, both got sentences. This time I didn't protest. I was a free man again and had some catching up to do.

Before the court case I found out that Mandy had given birth to a baby girl. Sadly, by the time I got out of prison, she was in a relationship with someone else. I was gutted but I could hardly blame her. I'd been off the scene for some while and even when I was around I didn't give her a lot of attention. I moved back into Sue's place and immediately began to make up for lost time. It was straight back to the old routine: getting stoned and burgling again, but now I was more confident than ever. I was really casual and fearless, and always on the look-out for buildings to burgle. Day or night I would climb up onto the roofs of buildings to work out how to get in and out and where the alarms were, often watching as police cars drove by. I would nearly always carry a weapon in case of a surprise. If I stepped into a silent beam by mistake and set the alarm off I would get out of the place and away as fast as I could, often just as the police car with sirens blaring arrived bringing sniffer dogs. I would just move on to look for the next job for the night without worrying about it.

One day a bloke I didn't know very well but used to smoke with sometimes had a huge amount of amphetamine. He offered me a line and I didn't refuse. He was a weird guy – the speed made him paranoid. Before he ever drove anywhere in his car he would virtually take it to bits looking for bugs he was convinced the drug squad had planted. He gave me a few ounces of the amphetamine to sell. A few days later the drug squad busted me, found the bag which I had hidden behind a bath panel, and arrested me. I was charged and remanded back to Armley prison to await trial again. This time there was no doubt in my mind that I would get stung when my hearing came up.

Armley lived up to its reputation as a pit from hell. But this time I knew the score and I didn't feel particularly bothered that I was locked up again. I knew a few lads on the wing from my last visit and the next day, during exercise, I met up with a few mates from my area. The days turned into months as I waited for my Crown Court date. I had enough magazines and books to pass the time: usually porn magazines and books on the unexplained and the paranormal. I was fascinated by witches and the devil and I spent many of the long hours in my prison cell brooding on the dark side. I knew that I had it within me to do some real damage to someone who crossed me – even kill them. Eventually the date came up. It was at Leeds Crown Court again.

This time my barrister told me to expect a custodial sentence, which was cool with me. Standing in the dock facing the judge I knew there was no escape and I would just have to take it on the chin. I swallowed hard as he read out my crimes one by one. Then finally I got my smack on the knuckles: two and a half years for burgling a house and a factory, stealing a car and possession of drugs. I was actually happy; I knew I should have got a lot more. The next morning as a newly sentenced prisoner I was taken in front of a board and told the name of the prison where I would serve my time. I was also told the earliest date when I could be released for good behaviour and the latest date I could be released. The sentence I had been given had been halved because it was under four years. If I was good I would serve half of it; if I kicked off and caused a stink, I would get some added on. I didn't care. If anyone cheesed me off they were getting a punch no matter what. I was nineteen and up for anything. I was given a date for my transfer; I couldn't wait to get out of Armley.

The date wasn't far away, but in the meantime my cell mate and I hatched a plan to get some extra drugs in. I wasn't really getting any visitors (or any mail for that matter), so we arranged that on the weeks when he wasn't due a visit, his friends would come and visit me. That way we would have gear every week. It was simple: he gave them my name and prison number and told them what I looked like. The following Saturday I was escorted to the visiting room. It was packed; there were officers everywhere, patrolling up and down. My name was called and I was given a table to sit at. When my visitors came in, we greeted each other and chatted even though we were complete strangers. After a while I asked them how big the package was. There are three ways in which a package, which is always wrapped in a condom or a balloon, can be handed over. If the visitor is a woman and she has the package in her mouth you can reach over and kiss her, and she passes it from her mouth to yours. You swallow it and it is safe. You get the package a few days later when it has passed through your body. The second way is called "plugging". Somehow the package is passed to you and you quickly reach down into your trousers and push the whole thing up your backside. Amazingly, it stays there and you can walk and even jump up and down. The advantage of this method is that you have immediate access to it back at the cell. The third way is just to stuff it down your pants or in your sock, but this is very risky as everyone is searched after a visit. On this occasion I used the third method. The transfer was successful and I made it through the searches. Escorted by officers I walked back very calmly to my cell with the rest of the lads who had had visits. As I approached my cell on the landing I knew we were OK. The last few nights before I left Armley to begin serving my sentence my cell mate and I were stoned out of our minds and happy to be sharing the cell together.

✛ ✛ ✛

My morning to move had come. I said my goodbyes and was sorted out with some weed for the journey. My destination was HMP Everthorpe in East Yorkshire, which was miles and miles from anywhere I knew. After an hour we arrived at Everthorpe which is in the middle of some woods. As usual we had a good laugh on the journey there. There were a few of us who were new and didn't know what to expect. Most of us were happy to be going to a working prison because it meant no more being banged up twenty-three hours a day and no more slopping out with the bucket every morning. We would have a job to occupy us during the day.

Everthorpe looked the same as any prison – high walls, razor wire, locks and bars – but it was not as antiquated as Armley and had a couple of new wings. After having the usual strip search, shower and being reminded of the rules, we were given our bed rolls and told to follow the officer. The place was massive. After going through a gate we walked along a wide corridor which must have been a quarter of a mile long. Inmates had nicknamed it the M1! As we walked along we passed lads on their hands and knees with big scrubbing brushes and blocks of soap, scrubbing away and polishing. "You're next," they shouted at us as we passed by. Everyone had to scrub the M1 at some point.

We were shown into the wing. I liked it immediately. It was small and clean and had a snooker table, pool table and a TV room. Our cells had actual toilets which was amazing! Every evening we were allowed out for about two and a half hours for what was called "association". When I walked in that first evening the whole landing was out and it was really noisy. Everyone was walking around as if they were Rocky Balboa: big attitudes and no smiles, staring at the new boys. It was all a show; all bravado and swagger designed to intimidate newcomers and put them in their place. But I knew full well that if you hit them in the right place they would scream like any man. I was afraid of no one and I made sure they knew it. Soon I got talking to some of the other lads who had also come from Armley and once everyone had flexed their muscles a bit, we relaxed.

I was waiting in the queue for a game of pool when the big gates at the end of the wing banged open and a load of lads coming back from the gym walked in, led by a screw. I didn't take much notice at first. Then, to my surprise, one of the lads walked up to the guy playing pool, snatched the cue out of his hand and said, "I'm on." I couldn't believe it: it was a bloke from Armley who I'd had a go at sorting out because he had been bullying and attacking a poor defenceless first-timer called Brownie who would never harm a fly. On that occasion, when I had confronted him just as exercise was ending, he had started mouthing off at me and had been pulled away by his mates. The issue had been left unresolved as far as I was concerned and I had made a mental note back then that if we ever met again I would grab a second chance to put him in his place. This was it! I stepped out of the queue and approached the table. Grabbing the cue from his hand I told him, "No mate, *I'm on*." The place went silent and everyone seemed to be watching, shocked. A couple of officers quickly came up to me and, jangling their keys, said, "Come on, Rowan. We don't want any trouble. Back to your cell to cool off." Everyone could sense a fight and I was gagging for it. As the officers manhandled me away, I shouted, "I'll bite yer f****** ear off in the morning," and I meant it. An hour later, when association was over and everyone was back in their cells, I heard someone banging on the ceiling of the cell underneath me and shouting. It was the same bloke. "See yer in the morning. I'm gonna bust yer up!" he threatened. I told him to stop running his mouth off and that action was guaranteed.

The next morning I woke early. I packed my toiletries in a bag and rolled up my bed roll. It was all part of the routine. I knew from experience that I would be dragged down to the strip cell on the segregation block for fighting, so I thought I might as well pack to go. The cell doors were opened and everyone started going about their business. Hearing a shout from below I looked down to see the bully dressed all in white, beckoning me to come down. He had two guys with him. I ignored him. I had seen all I needed to see. The white uniform told me that he was a servery boy. Dishing out the food to other inmates was one of the privileged duties.

Breakfast came around very quickly. Standing in the queue for breakfast I could see him serving and gradually, as the queue moved down, I got closer and closer to him. I picked up a metal tray to carry my food and held it close to me, refusing the first two breakfast choices as if I was waiting for something else. When I got close to the lad I let rip. "Come on!" I yelled at him swinging the tray to try to hit him in the face. Then I jumped up onto a nearby table, full of everyone's breakfast, sending crockery flying in all directions, and

54

launched myself over the counter towards him aiming a punch at his head. He backed off, startled by the ferocity of my assault. Alarm bells were sounding and whistles blowing as officers came flying from all directions and jumped on me. As I struggled against them, I could hear them shouting at all the other inmates to get back in their cells. I was so incensed that it took several officers to pin me to the floor. Two screws were holding my arms behind my back and two more were forcing my shoulders and head down on the floor. They dragged me all the way down the M1, threw me into a very dimly lit cell and ripped all my clothes off, at the same time landing me a good few punches. I was then made to wear a potato sack with the corners cut off for my arms to go through and a hole for my head. It was very dark and very quiet down there and I had no sense of time, apart from the fact that in the evening I was given a small, thin mattress and a blanket and in the morning they were replaced by a chair and a cardboard table. There was nothing else but me and the silence.

A few hours later I was brought before the prison governor and found myself in a mini court-room situation. Opposite me sat the governor with two officers on either side of him and another two officers were flanking me. An officer from the wing gave an account of my actions. I pleaded guilty and two weeks were added to my sentence, plus two weeks GOAD (Good Order And Discipline, which means being put in isolation for two weeks with only a dim light), plus loss of wages. Two weeks is a long time to be alone, but it passed and to my surprise I was put back on the same wing as before, but this time in a single cell. All of a sudden I seemed to have made a lot of friends. People would give me tobacco and send me spliffs (joints); they would smile and come and introduce themselves. Obviously I had won some respect. I saw the bloke who I had had the fight with and he just avoided me, which was cool by me. I had proven my point.

The next few months passed peacefully. As soon as I had had my gym induction, I was as happy as larry, working out either at the gym or alone in my cell. Everthorpe had an assault course which was a real killer. Along the way you had to do press-ups, sit-ups, squats – you name it – and you had to keep on going round and round. There was a bucket located mid-way along the course so you could puke up if you had to and then you just kept on going. After months of constant exercise I felt super fit. I had made a friend in the cell above me who provided me with regular supplies of cannabis, lowering joints down to me on a line. We would share spliffs and the line would go up and down all night until we were wasted. Apart from my daily job, all I seemed to do in prison was work out at the gym and get wasted.

Through the grapevine I heard that the whole prison was ready to kick off in a full-scale riot and wreck the place. I can't really explain the reason for planning the riot, and maybe there was no good reason. All I know is that when you are incarcerated, living on your wits, staring at the same four walls day in and day out, the frustration and anger is ready to boil over at any time – so why not riot? There were four wings to the prison, two at the bottom of the M1 and two at the top, in the shape of a letter I, with probably about 500 inmates. The signal to kick off would be given at association that night when someone on one of the wings would hit the fire alarm. All that day you could feel the anger brewing: all the hate and all the pain was ready to explode. Everyone was whispering about it and bragging about which screw they would take hostage or beat up. Weapons were made ready; pillow cases turned into balaclavas and hidden for the evening's events.

When work finished that day we were banged up in our cells for a roll check. We behaved ourselves as usual for tea and everything carried on as normal until association when everyone was waiting for the signal, distracting themselves by chatting about this and that. Some of the lads were planning on taking an officer's keys and trying to get out; others had talked about trying to make it to the prison hospital to smash open the drugs boxes and get high; others were just intent on smashing in the heads of people who had cheesed them off – the distraction of a riot would be the ideal time to mess someone up and do some real damage without getting caught. People who were in debt to others for tobacco or drugs were probably terrified that they would get done over. Maybe the officers sensed something was up because they seemed a bit nervous and edgy. Me? I was well hyped up and couldn't wait to let rip.

Maybe an hour passed of waiting and waiting for the bell to go. Everyone was getting very impatient – especially me. I was with a crowd of guys in the TV room at the end of the wing when we heard it ring. Immediately an officer came out of nowhere and locked us in the room – we were trapped. They must have guessed that trouble was brewing. Out on the landing everyone was going crazy: pool balls were being thrown, things were being smashed, everyone was waging their own private battle. Inside the TV room chairs were being thrown, all the lights on the ceiling were being smashed, glass was flying everywhere. I had lost it and was running from one side of the room to the other, screaming "Come on!" and "Kill!" and head butting the windows. We were in total darkness, but we could just see each other by the light on the landing. Everyone was getting the pent up frustration off their chest.

Suddenly, through the door in the corner we saw the riot squad coming running towards the TV room. They were loads of them, dressed all in black with helmets, truncheons and shields, some of them banging their truncheons against their shields. I knew then that they had known all along what we were planning. Someone had tipped them off and they had been waiting on standby in the gym. They outnumbered us significantly and they had a reputation for not messing around in these situations. We endeavoured to stop them from breaking in and getting us. Everyone started throwing chairs towards the door to make a barricade until there were probably forty or so chairs piled high. This was the only entrance in or out, so there was no escape. Totally frustrated, we turned our attention to ripping the hell out of the room we were in. When it was totally trashed, some sort of calm seemed to descend again. People began to flick on their lighters so we could see each other. Everyone was laughing, some out of a sense of exhilaration and some out of panic. Joints were rolled and passed round as a celebration.

I realized my neck was soaking wet and I reached up to touch it. Calling for someone to shine their lighter on my face and chest I saw that I was covered in blood. I had about a two-inch wide gash on my forehead and was losing a lot of blood. I ripped off my T-shirt and with help tied it round my head bandana style. After an hour or so the mood eased. Trapped and with no food or water we began to shout our demands to the riot team: we wanted to see the governor. Later we upped the ante and tried to demand a film crew and news team, as well as better food and more visits. But everything was refused. We were told that if we moved the chairs, the riot squad would stand aside and let us go back to our cells without any hassle; no more would be said about it and no one would be charged. We gave it some thought and eventually a few hours later we surrendered.

When all the chairs had been removed they called for everyone who was injured to come out, one at a time, with their hands above their heads. I was volunteered to go first as I was the only one injured. As I was escorted through the door and across the landing I caught sight of myself in a mirror on the landing wall. I was covered from my head to my waist in dried jelly-like blood and I still had my blood-soaked T-shirt tied around my head. I looked a real mess. Once inside the office I was told to lie down while my forehead was cleaned up and stitched there and then. Afterwards I was allowed a shower and locked in my cell. Everyone else had been taken to their cells one by one and locked up with no trouble. The mood was still tense, but by the next morning everything was more or less back to normal. Some people had been singled out as ring leaders and been told to pack their kit. They were taken to segregation or moved to other prisons. After that I was given the nickname "Two Smiles" because of the cut on my forehead, but most people called me "Jaffa" – a nickname I had picked up in the children's home. There was no real reason for it, it just stuck somehow.

The months rolled by. Fifteen months had passed quickly and my time for release was near. I was excited. I had learnt a lot more, made some good contacts and had already planned the things I wanted to do when I was out.

Chapter 4

On my release I was given a discharge grant because I was now twenty years old. I had also applied for a flat near where I used to live in an area called Brooklyn. I was taken to the train station and left there with another lad who was catching the same train. We were both buzzing. I knew that the first thing I was going to do was get wrecked and make up for lost time. I felt invincible. I had put on lots of muscle in prison and I wanted to use it.

Brooklyn was well known for drugs. You could get anything you wanted there: cannabis, speed, acid, pills, Ecstasy. There were at least eight blocks of high-rise flats, all quite close together. Nearly everyone knew that four or five flats in every block were drug dens, full of people getting high. I knew a lot of people there and so the first thing I did when I arrived back was to go visiting, leaving the keys for my new place uncollected at the housing office. All I wanted and needed to do was get stoned. My first port of call was my old mate Kenny's flat, which was always full of ageing hippies: big beards, long hair and off their faces. As usual, the room was filled with a dense cloud of smoke. Bongs (pipes) were being shared and pills taken; there were empty cans and bottles of drink all over the floor; inevitably there was someone strumming a guitar. Kenny was an eccentric. He had a dog called Monday because that was the day he had found it, and he used to get all his food from skips, picking up out-of-date tins of food which had been thrown out by some of the big-name stores. In fact, everything in his flat was found in skips or fields. Anything that looked weird or trippy would have its place – strange paintings, scruffy flamingos, headless dolls with flowers poking out of the neck. He was a complete extrovert and his knowledge of drugs was quite amazing. We became good friends.

It felt good to have my first very own place. It was a maisonette. I moved in and began to get things sorted. I'd only been on the outside again a few days when I bumped into a lad called Phil. We were to become close friends for the next few years; inseparable in fact. I had met him once or twice before but we hadn't really known each other very well – only by reputation. Now we just clicked for some reason and began hanging out together all the time. To be honest, Phil was a complete psycho with quite a reputation and had done some outrageous things. He wouldn't think twice about smashing someone's head in with an ashtray if they crossed him or even annoyed him. He had bitten people's ears off, stabbed others and could take several men down in a fight on his own, no problem. Wanting to get some gear for my new flat I started taking him burgling with me. I had become clever with alarm systems and now found most places easy to get into. There were plenty of buyers for stolen equipment and people keen to pre-order, so it didn't get long to get the flat in shape.

As soon as it was kitted out we started having parties. A couple of frequent guests were my old friends Andy and Nick, the brothers I first went to prison with. Many people brought speed (amphetamine) to the flat and we would consume ridiculous amounts of it. Often I would put a three-foot-long mirror in the centre of the room on the floor and would challenge people to compete for the longest "line" (i.e. with the powdered drug spread out in a long thin line). The person who could cut two separate lines on the mirror would always win. If we didn't snort it then we would inject it into our veins using a syringe. I had learnt how to hit my veins (I injected into my arm), how to cook the drugs up by heating it in a spoon. Drugs were usually snorted using a rolled up £5 note. Throughout the night our music blasted out and the amphetamines would give us so much energy that it would be literally days before we slept. The thing about speed is, if someone told you to run right round the world twice and be back for teatime, you'd believe you could do it! Usually we were so wired that when we eventually wanted to get our heads down, we would have to take some sort of sleeping pills and smoke plenty of weed. The rest of the people who lived in my block would complain about the noise from this man on the top floor who never slept and constantly partied, but I didn't care.

The speed parties at my flat lasted weeks. After going to a nightclub, sometimes gangs of people would come up to the flat to get high till morning. Because I lived on the very top floor, if you opened the bathroom window and stood out on the ledge you could feel for the roof, grab it with both hands and pull yourself up. It was a very dodgy manoeuvre because you were about 60 feet up! Once one person had made it, they could reach down and help pull up the others. In the daytime sometimes we would go up there, passing up the stereo, the speakers and the beer. If anyone had slipped they would have had no chance. With the music blasting out and our legs dangling over the edge we would get high. The police knew us well. They would shout at us to come down, warning us of the danger of falling on a child, but all they got in return was abuse. We didn't care. One day my brother Danny was on the roof with us and he had had too much to drink. In order to get him down from the roof we had to grab his hands, hang him over the edge and then swing him backwards and forwards until we had enough momentum to swing him into the bathroom window where someone was waiting to catch him!

One of the guys who was a regular visitor to my flat decided to buy a huge amount of speed and let us sell it for him. So I became a dealer in effect. Phil and I took the stuff from flat to flat, selling it and using it at the same time, leaving behind us a trail of flats all crowded with bodies getting high. When it was mushroom season, groups of us would go to the fields and spend hours hunting everywhere for magic mushrooms (some wild mushrooms contain the chemical psilocybin which gives a powerful hallucinogenic effect similar to LSD). I would usually go with Kenny the hippie. Even as you were picking them you would start to feel high as the drug seeped through your pores. When we had a few carrier bags half-full we would head home happy, knowing what the night had in store. At the flat we would sort them out and eat a few, boiling the rest and making cups of tea out of the juice. Then we would hold tight for the next six or seven hours while the effects kicked in. They blew your head clean off. If you had a bad trip you would start seeing devils or demons or start hallucinating. That was just tough: you couldn't stop it, you just had to sit through it. If you had a good trip, which I always did, it made absolutely anything possible. Everything seems to be moving; flowers in pictures turned into dancing women; the world was bright and beautiful. You can't speak; you don't feel human at all. Magic mushrooms make even the smallest thing like going to the toilet into a massive experience. All your senses are heightened; music becomes intense; your body is shaking; it can feel as if there are bolts of lightning going through your body. Sometimes it feels good, sometimes bad. It's hard to explain. Some people freak out or go over the edge.

Occasionally, we would pick fly-agarics, which are huge toadstools. They're the red ones with white spots that you usually see in children's books. They're poisonous and can kill you if they're not used properly. We would boil them in milk and then leave them to simmer. When they were ready, a gang of us would gather round to drink the liquor they produced; some bottled it. The trip was supposed to last about twenty hours. All I remember is that it was a very strange sensation.

Around this time we met a girl in our block who we became very friendly with and Phil and I would both have sex with her. In the block opposite there was another woman with three children who, like us, loved her drugs. The two of us would also go over to her place on a regular basis, get high and both have sex with her at the same time. We claimed her as ours. We were, therefore, not at all happy when one night we found another man with her. The first time it happened we asked him politely to leave, but the second time we threatened him with a Stanley knife to his throat and then chased him to his car wielding a baseball bat. It seemed the only way to get what we wanted was violence; people would listen to you out of fear.

Most nights I would go burgling and take someone with me. I preferred to work alone but on factories and office jobs extra hands were needed. We would find a huge office complex and either dismantle or disable the alarm or simply kick down the doors to gain entry into the building and take whatever we could find. Sometimes, after first breaking into the property, we would retreat for an hour or so to watch from a hiding place to see if the police came. If they didn't, we knew we were safe and we could take our time. Then we would move quietly from room to room, unplugging equipment and putting it near the door ready to transfer it to a safe place. To move it from the property, one person would stand on the opposite side of the road and wave you across when it was clear. Then it would be moved slowly, bit by bit, to its destination, usually somewhere local. We would only stop when it was light enough for us to be seen. A phone call at 6.00 a.m. to someone would mean, more often than not, that by 8.00 a.m. the buyer had come, bought the whole lot and was out of the area before the break-in had even been discovered. Sometimes it took longer, depending on the buyer. If the places we burgled were close to the flats, we would often bang on someone's window to let us in to hide the stuff in their flat till morning. No one argued with us. We said we would sort them out with some drugs in return and we did. We would spend the next hour rigging up six or seven computers, ready for the buyer to come. If we found cash in safes or cashboxes we would share it and use it to buy a few new clothes and a stack of drugs.

There were lots of burglars in Brooklyn and I had a reputation for getting rid of things, so people would come to us with their stash of jewellery, booze and electrical stuff and we would sell it – adding in a profit for ourselves, of course. Stealing had become everything to me. If I wanted something I would go out and get it. Anything that wasn't screwed down

I would steal. If I was passing a shop and there was a bike outside, I would jump on it and ride away. Even when I was in a store, I would pick up a bar of chocolate and start eating it or crack open a can of drink. I didn't care. One day a mate and I were out, miles away from our area, when I saw a tracksuit on a washing line. I stole it and put it on. Hours later, back in Brooklyn, I had just taken it off and put it in a cupboard when I heard screams from someone I knew. Two men were threatening to throw this bloke off the top of the block of flats if he didn't give them my address. As quick as anything the two men started running up the stairs towards me and there was a fight. One of them was the owner of the tracksuit I had taken earlier. He jumped on me, pushing me down onto the stairs and then pounced on me again, cursing loudly. As I attempted to get myself up, he fell on me again, landing heavy punches on me. I was being beaten. My mate ran to the next block to get some back-up but by the time he returned the two men had gone. I'll never forget that first time I was beaten. But it didn't change anything. I couldn't stop stealing.

During the day, while other people would be out window shopping for nice things, I would be checking out alarm systems on buildings and looking for ways to reach them. As evening fell I would be out on the job. It could be any place that we turned over, depending on where we were and what we were doing. Once we got onto the roof of a snooker hall and broke in. We ripped the backs off all the one-armed-bandits and emptied them; crow-barred the cigarette machines off the walls and stole their contents. We were even cheeky enough to get behind the bar, pull each other a pint of beer and take time to drink it before carrying on our way.

Sometimes, if I had missed a floor sensor in a building we were turning over, the alarm would go off and we would have to run, using short cuts and alleyways to reach safety, leaving police cars and the helicopter searchlight vainly scanning the area. Sometimes we had to run across streams to get the sniffer dogs off our scent and our hearts would beat wildly, but, gradually, as we put distance between us and the cops, we became calm and confident again, until eventually we slowed down to a walk and then we might sit down in the long grass in the pitch black to have a cigarette and chat about the next job for the night, watching while the police continued searching for us. The next job usually meant walking to the next town. Occasionally alarms would deliberately be set off at one end of the town to get all the police there, so that we could do another job at the other end of town. Clubs, shops, restaurants, warehouses, houses, cars, even churches: it didn't matter what type of place it was as long as there was something valuable inside.

Since whenever I was pulled up by the police day or night, they would search me for weapons, drugs or tools, I began to leave my "equipment" hidden all over town: screwdrivers in people's hedges, crowbars in the graveyard and wrenches on the roofs of shops I intended to burgle. Everywhere I went I had tools. Sometimes the police would arrive at the flat with a search warrant, kick the door off and turn the whole place over. More often than not I would be tipped off by friends living in other blocks who could see the police car coming and I would go underground, moving from flat to flat during the day and at night moving around via fields and railway lines.

If the police caught up with me I would always try and get away unless I could see that I was definitely cornered. I pulled some wild stunts to try and get away. On one occasion the police turned up when I was burgling a factory, so I took a flying leap straight through a window. On another, I had got in through the roof and had slid down a pole to the ground about 40 feet below, but when I hit the ground and walked around, the alarm went off. I ran to the first pole I saw and climbed back up, with the deafening alarm piercing my ear drums, only to realize that I had gone up the wrong pole. Clinging onto the pole with my hands and legs, I had to head butt through the roof in order to escape. When I got caught, as I did that time, I would always make it as difficult for the police as possible while they fingerprinted and photographed me. I saw them as my enemy; they stopped me doing what I liked doing. Facing the judge the following morning charged with three counts of burglary, I greeted him with a smile. I would always remain silent until I knew the verdict. If I got bail I would be silent, but if I got remanded into custody I would shout abuse. My solicitor put up a good fight for me. I had come to know the courts very well and I knew the maximum that they could give. On this occasion I somehow got a probation order for two years and was ordered to pay compensation. Angry that I had walked, the police vowed to put me down for a long time. I gave them the finger and carried on as usual. Getting high was all I knew and getting what I wanted seemed easy.

As well as drugs and burgling, another characteristic of our day-to-day life was fighting. I remember one evening we decided to go out to the pub. After an hour or so when I went into the toilet my mate and another guy came in after me and immediately a fight broke out. We beat the other guy up and left the pub straight away. The next evening a van of lads turned up armed with bats, banging on people's doors and looking for us. We were ready to take on any fight. If it happened, it happened. We didn't care. Somehow we escaped the confrontation that time. Another time we were sitting in someone else's room smoking when a local dealer from across the block came in and joined us. After a while, for no reason I walked across the room and gave him a right hook, knocking him out and leaving a hole where his head had hit the door. We thought this was hilarious and just carried on smoking while he recovered. After that the two of us actually became friends and I would regularly go over to his squat to smoke.

During one of our evening smoking sessions a bloke we knew quite well called Tim, who was a builder by trade, told us that he had managed to get a contract on a house and asked us if we needed work. We said yes and arranged to meet in the morning and go to the site together. After stopping for a cooked breakfast we finally arrived. The place was a mess: walls needed rebuilding, chimneys needed to be knocked down, electrics put in, and so on. It needed a lot of plastering work and it just so happened that my mate was a plasterer. As Tim was explaining the work that needed to be done, we stopped to snort a line and roll a joint. Eventually the work got started. Later that morning the owner of the house, who had a shop, brought over a crate of lager for our tea break and we got talking with him. When it became clear that he wasn't at all happy with the pace the work had been going up until then, my mate and I made out that we were professional builders and said that we would sack Tim and take over the contract. He wasn't very happy but he clearly didn't want to argue with us, so we went ahead. That evening we hired two of our friends to start work with us the next day, one to do the electrics, the other to roll joints and make up lines to snort. The guy we were passing off as an electrician had no idea what he was doing. He just pushed the wires into the wall without connecting them and put the case on, covering up the mess. That afternoon when the contract was signed we demanded half the money for materials and never went back.

With the money we went down to Bradford for a few days with the intention of scoring a big amount of drugs. Each day, after getting hold of the drugs in an area of the city that was buzzing with dealers all clamouring for any punter's attention, we would go down to the park to roll up and then make our way to a strip club where the stripper alternated with a topless female DJ. The stripper would get people to go up on stage with her and then take their clothes off. We would stay for a while and then, half drunk and stoned, we would go on to the next club, before catching a taxi home to carry on into the night.

I knew the police were after me again. I had been charged with assault with intent to resist arrest but had failed to surrender. I was also on a final warning from the probation office for failing to turn up to my regular appointments. I needed to tread carefully because I knew the police would have me in and remanded into custody before my feet could touch the ground. They wanted me desperately because they knew I was responsible for a lot of crime in the area. By this point the council had had enough of my neighbours' complaints and was pressurising me to move to a block two down from where I lived, which I did. Although it was the smallest of the tower blocks it was the one where all the dealers lived. On the first floor there was a lad who dealt cannabis and opposite him there was someone who dealt acid and speed; on the floor above mine there was an ecstasy dealer. At night the block never seemed to sleep – there was a constant flow of people coming and going like there was in my new flat. My brother Danny had also moved in on the first floor.

My new flat was really weird. Whoever had had it before

me had decorated it with black carpets and black units, some very freaky hanging nets, huge psychedelic posters, and there were buddhas and joss sticks still hanging around the place. I got myself a dog as a new accessory for the flat – a vicious black Doberman called Duke. Leaning against the wall in the front room I had installed a human skeleton, clipped together with wire, which I had stolen from a biology lab. It had a rubber snake going through its eyes, a joint in its mouth, and in its hands (one of which was made from radio parts) it was holding a guitar. Stretched around its hands was cotton wool with plastic spiders mixed up in it. Occasionally I dressed it in clothes. I would joke to people that his name was Henry because when I'd dug him up that's what it said on the gravestone.

I was getting bored with smoking cannabis all day, so I started to get involved in the rave scene which was full on around this time. The first rave I ever went to was in Leeds. We went with a plentiful supply of acid tabs, speed and cannabis. The place was jam packed. After taking the acid and the E's (Ecstasy) I began hallucinating. There was so much energy rushing through my body that I just had to move. All I could do was dance. Everyone seemed to be crazy, dancing their own dance in their own little world; hundreds of people with glow sticks and smiley T-shirts. People would just come and hug you for no reason and start dancing with you. Lots of people were openly trying to sell their E's or their magic mushrooms. The music was so loud that everything vibrated, including your own body. Hours seemed like minutes. Every-one was blowing whistles, going crazy; all with huge smiles and gritted teeth, trying to say as little as possible because the music was the most important thing. The strobe lights flashed and smoke machines pumped relentlessly. After four or five

hours of this everyone spilled out onto the street with pupils that looked like dustbin lids, high as kites. Some people just didn't know what to do or where to go. Eventually somehow our gang got together and, still tripping, we made our way home in a taxi. Nothing seemed real. I felt like I was charged with 2,000 volts of electricity. Without anyone knowing I had taken more Ecstasy and the inside of the taxi seemed to be melting before my eyes, the windscreen was wobbling like cellophane and the roads seemed to be painted in luminous colours. I couldn't look at the driver: his face looked oversized and extremely weird. Once home we smoked joints and hallucinated for hours and hours, until eventually we took sleeping pills so that we could get some sleep. But we had a very long wait, passing pipes and bongs and talking. The next day I felt as if the world was on my shoulders. So immediately the speed was out again to numb the depression and get me through another day.

After that I went to many raves. Dancing for hours on end left me very skinny and the days and days high on drugs were taking their toll, but I didn't care. I had decided long ago that death was a friend and had actually tried a few times to overdose, but my body had built up such an immunity to drugs that it didn't have the desired effect.

One night, having emptied yet another warehouse of its contents, this time on the other side of town, we stowed the gear at the flat of one of the gang I smoked with and hung out with because they lived nearby. The following morning, since we were having problems getting a buyer for all the TVs, computers, faxes, printers and camcorders filling my mate's bedroom, we went to a nearby town to try and find one. We put the word around and left our home address with a bloke we knew. Later that day a man in overalls turned up at our flat to look at the gear. We explained that it was at the other end of town and climbed in his mini to drive there with him. When we arrived at our mate's house, he wasn't in, so we got the buyer to wait at the front while we went round the back to kick the door off its hinges. When we opened the front door our buyer had momentarily disappeared – supposedly he had popped to the local shop while he was waiting for us to let him in. But seconds later a number of cars screeched to a halt outside the flat and the Regional Crime Squad was all over us. They came charging in front and back, screaming and shouting. We were surrounded, caught red-handed. We had been set up, and our supposed "buyer" was suddenly nowhere to be seen. We were cuffed and taken to the station where we were thrown in the cells spitting and shouting. It was becoming a regular thing.

I knew the police would ask for a three-day lie-down, which means being required to stay at the police station for three days of questioning about the job they have arrested you for and many others. They had waited a long time for this. I had been through the routine loads of times before and, as usual, I gave the CID as much stick as I could, refusing to answer their questions and just saying "no reply". In one interview, I have been told, I even tried to bite the microphone off the wall and on many occasions, if I could reach it, I would turn the tape off. The police hated me and I hated them. Most times I would be charged regardless to give the police time to gather their evidence. During the three days in the cells I would often be woken during the night for interview and questioned about all sorts of things. Those were long days, sitting in a dimly lit cell, never knowing what time it was. I would kick the doors and shout to my mates in the cells next door. Sometimes I would be asked nicely to be quiet and I would then ask for ten minutes in the exercise yard, which on occasion would be granted. The yard, which was covered by a cage, was tiny. You could only walk round so many times before you began to feel dizzy and you had had enough. It didn't take long for withdrawal to kick in and three days of going without drugs seemed like an eternity. I would feel sick, depressed and weak but I wouldn't let anyone see it. Sleep was the only way out.

On the third day of the lie-down I was handcuffed and taken to reception to wait to be transported by van to court. My mate Alan, who I had been arrested with, was brought down soon after. He was looking none too good either – probably the same as me, if only I could see myself. We were loaded into one of the newer "horse-box" style vans which were divided into tiny one-person cells made of solid steel, but each with a reinforced-glass window so that you could still see one another. There was a lot of shouting while everyone greeted one another and asked the usual, "What've you been caught for?" Although people were making light of it, underneath there was a lot of tension wondering what the outcome of the day would be. It never took much to light the touch paper. On one trip I remember everyone was so hyped up that when the van stopped at some traffic lights we all pushed on the same side of the vehicle to try and push it over. We almost managed it too.

When we arrived at court we were taken in two at a time and put in the holding cells, some in three-man cells and others in the cage. You always had to wait hours until your case was called. By now the jailers knew our names and we knew theirs. As the morning wore on the police came to let us know they were there and we were given the option of seeing our solicitors if we wanted to. Everyone did. For a start it was a chance to get some tobacco – and if your brief didn't give you some you'd usually sack them. We usually asked them to give us a shot at bail. I had had the same solicitor for a long time and he always laid it on the line for me, telling me whether or not I had realistic a chance at bail. This time he didn't hold out much hope.

When it was my turn to go before the judge I went up handcuffed to a bloke who told me that, if he got remanded, he was going to slip his handcuffs and make a run for it. Many people in the past had tried to jump over the dock at court and make a run for it past the judges or solicitors to the door. No one I knew had ever made it. In court, my solicitor put up a good fight for conditional bail, which meant a curfew and being forced to reside at one address, plus signing in at the police station every three days at a certain time. I never stuck to it anyway. But, along with my co-accused, I was remanded into custody. Since the prisons were all full, they stuck us in container units at local police stations where we stayed for the next couple of months, going back to court every fortnight to be remanded. Each time we went back to court we were refused bail until, a couple of months later, the case was committed to Crown Court for sentencing. I think there were about five of us in a line in front of the judge and a courtroom full of barristers, prosecutioners and onlookers, waiting for sentencing. After our charges and a summary of our backgrounds were read out, which seemed to take ages, we were finally sentenced. It was judgement day. With my record I thought I would definitely go to prison for a long time, but somehow, when sentencing was passed, to my surprise I was given 180 hours of community service. I couldn't believe it. I don't think any of us went to prison that day. That night we had a huge party to celebrate our freedom and the next day I was out burgling again.

One night I decided to go to the pub with a friend, which was unusual because I had many enemies in the area. We were sitting drinking when we heard a woman scream, "That's him!" Realizing she was referring to me and liking the look of what I saw, we got chatting with her and discovered that she used to be a hairdresser and recognised me from cutting my hair. Her name was Jenny. After talking for a while she announced that she was on night shift and had to go back to work. She and a couple of mates had sneaked to the pub during their break. She asked if she could borrow my jumper saying she was cold. When I gave it to her, leaving me bare-chested, she ran off down the street towards the factory laughing, taking my jumper with her, and I gave chase. As I walked through the factory in just my jeans and shoes looking for her, I got some very strange looks from the people doing their work on the machines. Eventually I found her, retrieved my jumper and left. It was the start of an unusual relationship.

The next day there was a knock at my flat door. I opened the door and there to my amazement stood Jenny. How she got hold of my address, I have no idea. I invited her in and she told me she had been sacked from her job. Her boss had discovered she'd been skiving off down the pub and when I came looking for her half-naked it hadn't helped matters. Jenny was strolling around my flat making herself at home and without warning she opened my bedroom door which was full of stolen goods. She said she knew I was a burglar and wanted to help me sell the stuff. Little did I know at that moment that we would be together for years to come in a stormy love-hate relationship. After a few days we began seeing each other and then I began going to her place and staying the night. We would smoke cannabis and snort and turn it into a red block of thick liquid which ran up and down the foil, depending on where you moved it with your lighter. When it was finished all that was left was a trail of burnt black lines. The first time I took it, it was a strange feeling but I liked it. I could hardly move; I felt relaxed and sick at the same time. I was with a group of other people all shooting up together. I looked around and saw that everyone else had also finished theirs; their heads were down with their chins on their chests, eyes closed. Little did I know that in a year's time everyone I knew would have an addiction to heroin.

I started going to Bradford in search of the drug and found plenty of dealers – but you had to watch out: there was a lot of dodgy stuff which was just powder in wraps. There were plenty of people who were out to rip you off. One time I was driven to the other side of town to meet someone that didn't exist and left there. On one visit to Bradford I managed to buy some crack cocaine and discovered I liked it a lot. It was new and different, very strong and very addictive, in fact deadly addictive. But you didn't get much of it and it didn't last long. After a few minutes it left you hyperactive, then snappy because you wanted more. When I could get it I would buy heroin. In Bradford there seemed to be more prostitutes than usual on the street corners. Chatting to them it was obvious that nine out of ten of them needed their fix and were withdrawing. Heroin was slowly taking over and dealers were springing up all over the place. The people I smoked with also began to get the taste for it, including Jenny. Since it was very expensive, needles into the veins were used to gain maximum effect.

Through the day whilst drugs were being dealt from home, I would still be going out looking for properties to burgle.

Needing to feed my growing habit, in broad daylight I would break into houses all over the area, first knocking, then, if no one was in, kicking the door off its hinges. From the window of our flat I could see all the way up the street. If I saw someone go out who I didn't know, I would go and kick down the door of their flat in broad daylight and burgle it. I had no morals. I would steal money, jewellery and anything I could carry. I wanted heroin more and more. Every time I had money I would trade it for heroin.

Now in all the flats I went to people were mainlining the drug into their veins. Everywhere was littered with bloody syringes, dirty swabs, spoons with soot all over them, spent filters and dirty foil, where people had smoked it instead of injecting it. Inexperience led to many people missing their veins and their arms swelling like a golf ball, but determination not to waste the precious heroin meant that they would try another spot until the barrel of the syringe was empty. Some people would fall over on the floor shaking and sweating like they were having a fit. But no one was interested. All they cared about was getting their own hit. We all seemed to forget that heroin was addictive. Because it was new and available we all got caught up in the moment; but the moments turned to weeks and then you were hooked; it didn't take long. The whole atmosphere on the drug scene had changed; people were getting desperate for heroin. When I scored, I would keep it quiet, only sharing it with my close mates.

Jenny became pregnant. Around the same time we changed from dealing acid to heroin and crack. By now I knew I had a habit. I would wake up first thing in the morning sweating and then freezing with cold and in pain. I would be so desperate for a fix I could have killed for it. I knew I had a problem. A lot of my mates were the same. They would sell their clothes, their CDs, their stereos, TVs, gold rings – anything to raise £20. I've even seen people sell their wedding rings for one hit. If they ever had any self-respect, it was now gone. Everyone began to change. It was dog eat dog. You would try to find places to hit up where there were less people around in case they asked you for any. You would see grown men in tears, begging for one hit. But from the man with the powder there was no emotion. I would wait four or five hours, pacing up and down, for deliveries of heroin. To the addict, nothing else in the world matters; only that the heroin arrives and you get it. While doing community service ordered by the courts I would steal from the homes we were decorating. I couldn't stop. It was all I knew. Soon I had a prescription at the local chemist and was picking up Methadone on a daily basis to take the edge off the addiction.

A guy I knew, aware that we still had many customers from selling cannabis, asked us to deal heroin for him. I said yes and took a large sum of money off him to go and score. But all the money went on other things. Days later some people reported to Jenny and me that they'd seen some blokes kicking our door in, looking for me. A contract was out on my life and I knew these people meant business. As Jenny was pregnant we quickly moved out and set ourselves up in a new flat about five minutes away from our old place, but it wasn't long before they'd tracked us down and turned up on the doorstep. When the heavies showed up I wasn't there but they spoke to Jenny and threatened her. When I found out (even though I had taken and blown their money) I was so angry that I armed myself with a pump-action shotgun and went looking for the guy who had given me the money. Taking a backstreet route I went to a house where I knew he might be. I banged on the door but there was no answer. Carefully, I engraved his name on a live bullet and posted it through the letter box. His henchmen never came back.

Very soon after this Jenny and I bought a load of heroin from a contact in Bradford. I will never forget the estate where we got it, because it was worse than anywhere I had ever been – and all my life I had lived in some rough places. There were needles strewn literally all over the streets and burnt-out cars left abandoned all over the place. Most of the houses had steel shutters on the windows and doors to stop people getting in. The ones that didn't have this protection had been gutted, even down to the wiring which had been stripped out and sold. Standing on every street corner were small gangs and there was the constant roar of motorbikes flashing past. It was the first of many times that we went there to score heroin. Over a period of time we met a lot of people. It was a simple equation: they wanted our money, we wanted their gear. If we could rip them off, we would. And vice versa. I was careful and always took a pair of scales and a mirror with me when buying – scales to weigh the gear and a mirror to cut a line and test the purity of the heroin. I wouldn't hand over any money until I was sure I was getting quality gear. Sometimes, even before I left, I would have a hit. My habit was steadily growing.

By now Jenny was heavily pregnant. The night she went into labour her parents rushed her to hospital with me tagging along. After a while the midwife told us it would be some time, maybe another twenty-four hours, before the baby was born and suggested we go home and get some rest; they would call us when it was nearly time. On my way home I kept an appointment I had made with some guys who I wanted to buy a few hundred Ecstasy tablets off. On the top of a huge mirror we emptied out a large pile of amphetamine at one end and at the other end fifty acid and fifty diabetes capsules. Having emptied the contents of the diabetes capsules in the bin, we filled each capsule half with acid and half with speed and then shot down the motorway to catch people queuing up outside raves, most of whom would be looking for E's. We walked down the queues selling our drugs and then drove back up the motorway.

Later that night Jenny's mum rushed us back to hospital to see the birth of my daughter Roxanne. It was the most amazing thing that I had ever seen and she was a beautiful baby. I couldn't wait for them both to come back home. When they did, life resumed its normal pattern of scoring and burgling to get money to feed our habit. Jenny and I still had terrible arguments, but we always waited till Roxanne was in bed.

It was around that time that my friend Kenny died. It was a shock. I had never had a friend die before. Although he was a drug addict, it wasn't the drugs that killed him but cancer. Jenny stayed home with Roxanne while I went to the funeral, but I came home rather the worse for wear and we had a terrible argument. Jenny held our baby in her arms while we screamed and shouted at one another. I was out of control and had my hands around Jenny's throat, about to strangle her, when her mum called at the door. Hearing the screams she rushed in and pulled me off Jenny, screaming abuse at me. I left, drunk and confused, to find somewhere to hit up. After that incident Jenny's family hated me more than ever. I returned later that night and we got back together for a few months, but then there was another huge argument and I stormed out yet again. From the window Jenny screamed out that I would never see my daughter again. That broke me in two and I went on a burgling spree to supply myself with drugs and booze … anything to silence the pain. Once or twice I even drank methylated spirits. I was in more of a mess than I had ever been. All I wanted was heroin. I broke all my bail conditions and my community service order, even though I knew it would mean a long prison sentence. I couldn't take not seeing my child. My relationship was over. I was going back to prison but this time with a heroin addiction.

Seeing no future ahead, I decided to kill myself. This is what the rollercoaster highs and lows of drug abuse do to you. It's like you are stuck in a black hole which is impossible to climb out of. Hopelessness and paranoia set in and life seems cheap and worthless. I felt I had reached the end of the road and my life had spiralled out of control. Initially I tried to take an overdose of sleeping tablets but, as before, it didn't work – my body took whatever I threw at it. Then one day I walked past a derelict building and decided to investigate. It was dark inside and the windows were boarded up; it was full of rubbish and old furniture that people had dumped there. Walking around inside I saw a window ledge about four feet off the ground and, within reaching distance, a roof beam with a metal hook sticking out from it. I contemplated my death and surrendered to it. I wrote a note to Jenny and Roxanne, simply saying something like, "I am dead inside the building. Jenny, Roxanne, I can't go on. I'm sorry. I love you." I put the note in my hat and walked outside to lay it by the side of the road, quickly walking back inside. I climbed up on the ledge, took my scarf, which usually hid my face from the police, and made a noose. I sat on that ledge for about an hour or more in tears. I didn't jump. I got down and left. But the next day I returned more determined and found myself on the ledge again with the note outside. This time I had brought with me two scarves to tie together. Again I made the noose and climbed the ledge. I tied the scarves round the hook and put the noose around my neck. I thought my neck would break with the drop. Counting from ten I jumped.

In those few seconds so many things ran through my mind. My body was spinning and my legs were kicking wildly. I couldn't breathe and I had given up. I thought I had taken my last breath. But then I felt a huge thud. The scarves had snapped and I was lying on my side on the ground, having a fit. Gasping for breath I managed to pull the scarf from around my throat. In those seconds I heard very plainly whispering evil voices all around me. It felt like I was surrounded by about fifty people, all approaching me, getting closer and closer, but as I coughed and spluttered, finally getting my breath they withdrew and were suddenly gone. When I was finally able to stand and breathe I almost ran out of that place. Hours later I was back in a gloomy flat with a belt around my arm, injecting heroin into a vein with some of the usual crowd. A few days later Jenny and I got back together and life reverted back to its normal groove.

One night, returning from selling my stolen goods, I came round the corner to see our house swarming with the drug squad and police. Jenny was being busted and my little girl was also being taken into custody. Immediately all sorts of thoughts went through my head: Jenny would go to prison and Roxanne would be taken into the care of the local authorities. In fact, Jenny's mum applied for custody of Roxanne and it was granted to her. I knew that meant it would be very difficult for me to ever see her. Just as Jenny was released on bail I was arrested for house burglary, breach of probation and my community service order and also perverting the course of justice, which means threatening and interfering with witnesses. At court I was remanded into custody and so I was on my way back to prison. All the way there in my head I wrestled with the terrifying reality that I knew awaited me in prison: I knew I would have to withdraw from my drug addiction and it scared the hell out of me.

Chapter 5

When I arrived at the prison there was only one thing on my mind. Avoiding withdrawal at all costs. I had to get hold of some gear and I had to see the doctor. The majority of people coming into prison would be withdrawing from something and one by one we would see the doctor and be given a small DF tablet to take the edge off the withdrawal symptoms and a prescription to pick them up daily. They didn't work for me: my habit was too big – but it was better than nothing. After four or five hours in reception, bed rolls in hands, we were taken to our cells. My only hope was that my cell mate might have something – sometimes you could strike lucky. The prison was gloomy; you could cut the air with a knife because, as usual, it stank. My cell door was unlocked and I came face to face with the man I was going to spend twenty-three hours a day with for the foreseeable future. After the usual rather stilted conversation, I confessed my dilemma. He couldn't help me; he didn't have anything. There was nothing for it: I was going to withdraw.

I could already feel the sweat pouring down my face and

from my armpits. My nose was running. One moment I felt freezing cold and in serious pain like someone was stabbing me in the gut and continuously turning the knife. The next I was too hot and jumped off the bed and paced up and down; to try to cool down I pressed my body against the cold wall. I couldn't stay in one position for more than a few seconds. I lay on my bed wanting the earth to swallow me up forever, dreaming about just one more hit. I needed it; I wanted it. Every few seconds I experienced cramps in my legs and I kicked out in pain then curled up in a tiny ball again, clutching hold of my legs and massaging them to try and ease the pain. I lay naked on the cell floor by the toilet sweating, then felt freezing cold and put my clothes back on. So it went on, all night long. The night seemed to last forever. You shake and hallucinate. You feel like you're literally dying. You want to scream. You feel like committing suicide.

It wasn't just me, it was going on all over. In desperation some people would catch hold of a line as it passed by their cell window on its way to some other prisoner and steal the stuff attached to it, willing to take the consequences in the morning. Hours and hours pass by until you hear the birds singing and the morning staff jingling their keys as another day's routine grinds into motion. When the cell doors eventually open, as usual everyone shouts across the landing at one another, getting Rizlas or tobacco and passing on old newspapers or porn mags. There's always someone you know from your area or a previous sentence or an old cell mate. You can always tell who's withdrawing. They're the ones who, like me, are skinny, unshaven, smelly, white-faced, black-eyed and desperate: the living dead. Immediately your search for gear kicks in. For a few minutes you feel hopeful that someone might sort you out, but to no avail, and minutes later you're banged up again. There's one more chance in an hour's time during exercise – that is, as long as it's not raining. And if you don't have a phone card or tobacco to barter with, you're out of luck anyway, because that's your money. A tiny bag of heroin costs you three phone cards, worth £6, or the equivalent in tobacco. Pay day is usually Wednesday when you get around £4.20 for the week. Many people club together with their cell mate to get a tiny bag of heroin which lasts only minutes. Then you have to go the rest of the week with nothing. At exercise I found some lads who were able to sort me out on the condition that I gave them double back. Things in the prison seemed different than before. Now most people were hooked on heroin.

It was a whole week before I had my first visit at the prison. Visits stir up a whole range of emotions: excitement, anticipation, desperation, fear. The cell door opens and the guard announces, "Rowan, visit." The first thought that goes through your head is, "Will they have some gear for me?" because that's all that matters to you. You wait at the bottom of the stairs with a crowd of lads until it's time to be escorted over to the visiting room; there's usually a lot of banter and laughter. Everyone keeps a close eye on those who have visits in case they have something to sell when they come back.

The visit is always a very tricky operation because, of course, the officers know that there will be a lot of people trying to get drugs in, and they also know who is an addict and on medication and who has been caught before. So inevitably some people get caught. Arriving at the visiting area you're locked in a room and called out a few at a time, told to put on a bright yellow bib and given the number of the table each prisoner is to sit at. Walking into the visiting room is always an experience. It's full of about forty lads and their visitors, plus their screaming kids; it's very loud and smelly – but for once it's the pleasant smell of perfume. The lads shout across to one another. Everyone, apart from the officers of course, knows who's going to get what.

Still withdrawing and looking very ill, I sat at my table, watching as a new set of visitors came in. Jenny walked in – she'd got bail. She smiled as she walked over to my table showing me a parcel in-between her teeth. It was big and wrapped up in a condom. She leant over and kissed me, passing it from her mouth to mine. It was very quick. I looked left and she looked right. Had we been seen? No. We chatted for a while. I knew that if I swallowed the package it would take three days before it passed through me and I could get hold of it. As we chatted, suddenly the riot bell rang and about fifteen officers hurtled into the room towards a table, grabbed a prisoner by the throat so that he couldn't swallow and threw him on the floor. Then, with one officer on each arm, they marched him out to be strip searched. His visitors were immediately escorted from the building. At this moment, while all the focus was on this one poor bloke, everyone else "plugged" their gear. I'd got what I needed. There was still twenty minutes of the visit remaining but I couldn't wait. We ended the visit. I was searched and headed back to my cell with my gear intact. All the way back, I was asked, "You got anything for sale?" "No," I replied. Some people would smuggle in cash to buy gear and that money would in turn be smuggled out to buy more drugs. Standing outside my cell, waiting for the guard to open it, all I wanted to do was get inside. I'd told my cell mate through the crack in the door that I'd got it and he was already preparing the foil to smoke it on. It had been seven or eight days since I last had a fix. All that time I'd been withdrawing. Now I was sweating because I had what I needed. The officer came to let me in. My cell mate and I both deliberately looked sad. He was lying on the bed pretending to read his book. As soon as the door was closed and we heard the keys slowly turn, we cheered and laughed. My cell mate stood at the door listening until I had retrieved the package. We washed the bag, then we took some heroin out and split it before wrapping the rest up again and re-plugging it. It was only minutes before we were smoking our heroin.

Ten minutes later the people in the cell above us were banging on the floor for us to come to our window. They had sent down a note lowered on a line, asking if we had anything for sale and a list of things they had to offer. The guys on our left and on our right also started banging on their wall and sent notes. I never sold unless I had to. As the night wore on we made cups of tea for ourselves. Since there is no hot water or a kettle in your cell you have to be ingenious. We made hot drinks by connecting two wires to each end of a razor blade, pushing the wires into a plug socket then dropping the razor blade into a cup of water. When the plug is switched on you wait and eventually the water boils. We knew the gear we managed to get would only last a few days. Then the withdrawal symptoms would start all over again.

Another way we got drugs was when we appeared at court to have our remand reviewed. While you, the prisoner, were standing in the five-foot-high see-through dock, handcuffed to a police officer, two people who had come to court to "support" you would approach, ostensibly to ask a question of the officer. While one distracted the officer, the other would pass you gear through an inch-wide gap in the dock. The first time I went back to court on this latest stretch, on the journey back, having successfully received another package of drugs, I ended up fighting some lad I didn't know and we had to be separated. That meant that, even before I had been sentenced, I had extra days to be added on.

Back at the prison I was given a different cell, but my new cell-mate and I just didn't get on. It was one of those things – it often happened. He was forever whingeing on about his family and the fact that he couldn't cope and, since I didn't feel that anyone in my family gave a toss about me, he really wound me up. One night I woke him up with a razor to his throat, telling him that I didn't want him in my cell. In the morning, when the doors were opened for breakfast, I threw all his stuff out onto the landing and gave the officers an ultimatum: they either needed to put me in solitary or move him. They did neither, so we were lumbered with each other. A few days later he told me that he wanted to commit suicide. I handed him a razor and told him to go ahead: I assured him it wouldn't hurt. While he sat staring at the razor I hung out of my cell window, giving my next-door neighbours a running commentary on my cell-mate's near-death movements. Gradually a whole load of people started chanting, "Do it, do it!" He didn't have the bottle, so after some time he asked me to do it for him. I took hold of the razor and, while he held out his wrists, I slashed them and the blood started spurting everywhere. I quickly threw the razor out of the window and started kicking my cell door. Five minutes later the door was flung open and some officers appeared. They led him out, with his arms raised above his head. When they asked me what had happened, I just told them that he had slashed himself. Left alone in my cell, I mopped up his blood and carried on with life as if nothing had happened. The bloke didn't die, by the way. He had stitches and was placed on a protection wing. The next day I had a new cell mate.

Not long after this I was due a visit and I was expecting more drugs. As usual the cell door opened and I was escorted over to the visiting room, waited, was given the yellow bib and then a table number. After a few minutes Jenny walked in. We greeted one another and she told me she had a package for me. We were very close to the guard who was supervising the whole room, sitting on a chair on top of a table scrutinizing all the visitors, so we needed to wait for the right moment. The minutes ticked by. Time was running out and I was beginning to feel desperate. If I didn't get it now, I never would. The officer knew me and was keeping a close eye on me. For one second he turned his head. Jenny passed me the package and I quickly put it in my mouth. At that instant the alarms began ringing and, about three feet away from our table, a door burst open and five or six officers charged in and pounced on me. One had his hands around my throat to try and stop me from swallowing the package. I was thrown to the floor and then dragged out, kicking and choking as I desperately tried to swallow – but since the package contained around twenty-five tablets wrapped in cellophane, it was big. Eventually I managed it. In the strip room my trousers were pulled down to check if I had anything hidden. Back in the visitors' room I could hear screaming and shouting as Jenny struggled with a woman officer before being escorted out of the prison. With my hands locked behind my back I was taken off to solitary for a proper strip search. By tea time I was back in my cell, having been charged with smuggling. As soon as I got in my cell I mixed shampoo with water and drank it quickly to try and make myself throw up. But it didn't work. Luckily my cell mate already had quite a lot of heroin, so at least we would be able to sleep for a few nights.

Every day, in or out of prison, seemed to be a race against

the sun – a race to get something so you would be able to sleep. The next morning, as well as having twenty-eight days added to my sentence, I was put on "closed visits" (which meant that during visits you had to sit behind a screen and no one could touch you) and got GOAD (isolation) for five days.

Shortly afterwards my big day arrived for trial at Crown Court. Since I was pleading "not guilty" on some of my charges I had spent a lot of my spare time trying to study my depositions in preparation for court. One particular undercover detective had joined the long list of officers who had vowed to lock me up for a long time. I knew I would have to face him in Crown Court before a jury. The atmosphere on the journey down was tense; some of the men were anticipating being put down for a long time. I saw my barrister and he told me it wasn't looking good. The police had witnesses who were ready to testify. I knew I was guilty but it was up to them to prove it. I would try anything I could to push the system to its boundaries. Why not? There might just be a chance that I could get off. It only took about an hour for the jury to find me guilty with a unanimous verdict. Once again I was told that I was a menace to society before being given eighteen months consecutive for perverting the course of justice, burglary and breaches and moved to a different prison. Since I was expecting five years, as far as I was concerned it was a good result and I left the court a happy man. Although it was a couple of hours' drive away, in the middle of nowhere, it was a working prison like Everthorpe and at least it meant no more twenty-three-hour-a-day bang-up.

In this prison you could wear your own trainers and there were more drugs than I had ever seen behind bars. I immediately hooked up with some old mates who filled me in on the score. Each evening at 7.30 p.m., everyone had to return to their cells and the gate at the end of the corridor would be locked. But all the cells – about ten in each corridor – were left open. This was new to me. It meant that we could do what we wanted all night. It was good: we could go in and out of each other's cells, smoking dope and playing cards, with music blaring out. No more swinging lines for Rizlas or matches. However, if you got into a fight you were on your own because there was no officer to break it up and occasionally it could get really vicious. Most of the time it was alright, but now and then something would erupt. It was normally as a result of bullies demanding trainers or other things from people who couldn't handle themselves very well. If it was someone's last night in prison it was always chaos. Everyone would pin the poor bloke down and carry him, struggling and cursing, to the gate at the end of the landing where, with everyone cheering loudly, he would be spread-eagled onto the prison gates and tied by his hands and legs. Then buckets of cold water – and perhaps the rubbish bin – would be thrown all over him. Sometimes the bloke's eyebrows would be shaved off, and even his hair, and toothpaste would be smeared all over him. Then he would be left there for a while. It was great entertainment! Occasionally one of the officers would come in and laugh with us, telling us to make sure we cleaned the place up later. Some of the lads took it in their stride, just glad to know that they would be free the next day, but others were terrified and pleaded with the officers to let them spend their last few days in prison in segregation.

Every Saturday morning you had inspection. One of the officers would shout, "Stand by your beds" and then they would come round to see if your cell was tidy. If it wasn't you would be punished – both by the officers and by the other inmates, who branded you as a scruff. After being at the prison a week each prisoner would be given a job. Having managed to get a job in the gardens I was moved to another wing. Luckily some lads from my home town who I knew managed to get me on their wing. Later that day during exercise, as I walked around the yard, I was amazed to see people standing round the edges in gangs selling smack and weed. Apparently the wing I had moved into was the main source of supply for almost the whole prison and the blokes there weren't to be messed with. When they were withdrawing they were desperate and for a fee of just £10 would slash someone's face open with a razor blade to settle a grudge. That night at bang-up I was introduced to the rest of the guys on our quarters and we rolled joints and chatted together for most of the night.

When I started my job on gardens the next day, my mates showed me the ropes, including a little scam they had going, smuggling eggs from the prison's 2,000 chickens back to the wings. Once I had managed to steal a metal tray from the prison kitchen I would regularly cook scrambled eggs for the rest of my corridor for supper, lighting a fire by burning bed sheets. It was a great way to get myself in with the lads. After a few weeks I was given some gear to sell and was trusted 100 percent. Money, tobacco, phone cards, food, gold rings and stereos were offered daily in exchange for drugs. Now and again the whole landing would be raided by a posse of officers who swooped in, tipping up beds, pulling out drawers and basically ransacking the whole place, searching for gear or evidence of dealing. If anything was found, the person under suspicion would be moved first to the segregation block and then to another prison. We called it "the Ghost Train". It meant you had to be really careful about how much gear you had at any one time. Anything more than a tiny amount and they would say you were dealing. Most of the time, however, they didn't find anything as during the day all gear was plugged and just taken out when needed. Generally, it would only be stashed somewhere in the cell if there was too much of it, which happened occasionally.

Christmas was approaching, so one evening we got together to plan ways to get in the maximum amount of drugs we wanted, working out in fine detail how much we would sell and how much we wanted for our own personal use. A tattooist had recently turned up in the jail and he was doing tattoos for people in exchange for gear. While he was working they would play really loud music to drown out his tattoo gun and someone would keep watch. We hired him to come to our corridor to give someone a tattoo so we could take a look at his work. Satisfied, we paid him to make us our own gun, which he did out of a tape recorder motor, sewing machine needles and a bent spoon, all taped together and wired into the electrical socket in the cell. We then stole Indian ink from the art room on the Education block and each evening we would spend hours smoking joints and tattooing one another. I got mates to tattoo devils and skulls all over my body: my chest, my arms, the backs of my legs, my knee caps, my feet, my head, everywhere. It passed the time while we were high. It was my way of rebelling against the prison and the world and for those reasons alone I enjoyed it. Sometimes I would take the gun and tattoo myself just for fun.

The day all the Christmas visits were due to take place was full of tension and excitement. Everybody was expecting something. The day passed smoothly, despite the fact that all the officers were extra sharp. That evening after lock-down all the drugs came out. We had a stash of 100 Ecstasy pills,

6oz of weed and huge amounts of heroin, cocaine and bicarbonate of soda. We hid most of it and then spent the rest of the night getting stoned and cutting around forty £10-wraps to sell. Our stash lasted us for the whole Christmas period. In the early hours of the morning we would make freebase crack cocaine ("rocks") with the coke and bicarb and, still constantly tattooing one another, talk about "release". Each of us would tell stories of run-ins with the law and boast about how to beat the system, which, looking back, seems crazy seeing as every single one of us had been caught – and most of us more than once!

On Christmas Day I tried to make contact with my daughter Roxanne. I rang the house and she picked up the phone, but as soon as my mother-in-law realized it was me she slammed the phone down. I was wounded and got loaded to ease the pain. In my heart I always dreamed that if only I could start again, I would do this or that different: be a better dad, never use drugs again. I was always wondering, "What if this hadn't happened?" or "What if I had done that differently?" It was the secret side of me that no one else knew anything about. Inside I knew I was a lost soul. I questioned the path my life had taken and struggled to see if it could ever, possibly, have meaning and purpose. Whenever I visited this "place" inside I always ended up feeling worse than ever. The fact was I could never change the past ... It just wasn't possible. But could my future be any different? I wasn't sure it could.

Christmas passed quickly. Since it was blatantly obvious that many of the lads on our corridor were high and hallucinating we were busted. Our cells were turned over and dogs were brought in to sniff around, but they didn't find anything. Someone on the look-out for an early release date had grassed us up. When the rest of us found out who he was, he would be in for it – no mercy shown. Nine times out of ten it was someone who had borrowed so much gear that they realized they couldn't pay, and so their only remaining hope was that their supplier might get caught and be moved to another prison wiping out their debt (every week whatever anyone owed was doubled). The way they usually did it was to stick a note under the office door telling the screws where the drugs were. It was a regular occurrence. Nothing was found on our landing, but after that we laid low for a few weeks, only getting the gear out at night. Meanwhile we loaned our tattoo gun out to another part of the prison for safekeeping in exchange for some "home brew" made from yeast, sugar, apples and sultanas, which had been on the go for months. All the ingredients had been stolen from the kitchen and brewed in bleach bottles so it had a pretty hefty kick – and not just from the alcohol content.

Although there were so many drugs in prison, it was a lonely place and the days went by very slowly. My mind was constantly consumed with evil thoughts and fantasies. One of my favourites was thinking about whom I would kill, either by stabbing them or shooting them. I would spend hours thinking about the people who had hurt me and imagine myself taking my ugly revenge. I didn't know who I really was. I just thought that the person I had become was the person I really was, and that was that. I didn't think a person could change. So many people had told me that I was bound to end up doing life in prison at some point that I just believed it. Prison didn't seem a punishment any more. I accepted that it came with my choice of life and couldn't be helped. In a way I felt secure there; I knew the system. The moment I arrived back, I would begin to plan for my release: bigger crime, better crime. There's no doubt about it that most times when the police caught me I was nearly already dead from the drug abuse. So in a way prison saved me. They were doing me a favour. By the time I was released I had built up my strength again and was ready to go. I wasn't at all interested in coming off drugs and getting clean. I felt alone in the world. My family was all divided and broken up, full of hatred. If you took crime and drugs out of my life there would be nothing left – it was all I had; it was the only thing I was any good at.

Chapter 6

My eighteen months in prison were coming to an end. It felt like a long time since I'd last tasted freedom. If it hadn't been for my gran and my aunt offering for me to go and stay with them I would have been homeless when I got out. I had lost the flat when I had been sent down again. My gran and my aunt were the only two people in my family who meant anything to me – they were my rock. I didn't see them very often but I knew they really cared about me and I always knew that they were there for me.

The weeks turned to days. Since on the final countdown it became tougher to get drugs into the prison, we had to use other methods. Some of our mates on the outside, knowing we were desperate for gear, would drive up to the prison wall, skid to a halt, throw a tennis ball loaded with gear over the fence and shoot off again. Somehow, some way, we would always get our gear. We needed it just to get ourselves through another day.

The night before my release I shaved my head and had it tattooed for a bet. It was my way of sticking two fingers up at the world. In the morning my head was still bleeding, but what the heck! I enjoyed the buzz of wondering whether they would let me go or keep me in – either way I didn't really care – but in fact the officers were only too pleased to get rid of me. They chucked me out bald and bleeding.

It felt good and strange at the same time to be free: the smells, the noise, the busy road, everyone rushing around. No bars, no officers. Being able to go wherever I wanted to. I loved my gran and my aunt and was grateful for somewhere to stay where I was genuinely loved, so for a couple of days I stayed at home. Inside, however, I was bursting to go out and get high. On the third day I could hold out no longer and I made my way back to Brooklyn. Within an hour of leaving Gran's, I was cooking up heroin on a dirty spoon, ready to shoot it into my arm. I was in the flat of an old mate who had been happy to see me and to share his gear with me. Coming round after my hit I can remember looking at everyone sprawled half dead around the filthy flat and thinking to myself that everything was OK again. I was free and I was high. My mates filled me in on all the important things in life, like who was dealing, who had the best gear and who had died of overdoses recently.

That night when I returned to my gran's, completely smashed, I knew I had let her and myself down. But I was past caring. From then on every day was the same. I was back in the same old groove. One night I broke down in tears and confessed, showing my gran my bruised arms full of holes. I couldn't understand why I was doing this to her. It was probably the first time I had cried in years. My Aunt Cheryl, who was a nurse, was visiting my gran at the time and she invited me to go and stay with her, miles away from the area, to try and withdraw from heroin. I agreed. During the day, while she was at work, I would be alone at home trying to sweat it out. In an effort to take my mind off withdrawing I would walk round the area looking for houses to burgle or cars to steal. Despite her real care for me, in the end I couldn't take it any longer and one day, without warning, I left. I needed some gear and some action. I couldn't hold out any longer: the pains and the cramps were too much.

Back in Brooklyn I met up with my old mate Andy and we got high together. He told me that the week before he had attacked a dealer and was planning to have another go at him. That was the way it was going now. People were using violence to get what they wanted and it was getting very nasty. I volunteered to go with him and help. So, armed with a hammer, we made our way to his place. Because the dealer knew Andy, he waited round the corner while I went in to do the business. The plan was to ask for a big weight in gear and, when it was on the scales, pull out the hammer, do the necessary and get out unscathed. But as soon as I was inside the house I saw that I was well out-numbered. There were eight other people in the room all smoking. I blagged my way out of the situation by asking for a ridiculous weight of gear, which I knew they wouldn't have, and got out as fast as I could. We spent the rest of the afternoon knocking on doors, pretending to be window cleaners looking for work, trying to find a house we could break in to. Eventually we found one and stole as much as we could carry. Once we had sold it all, we got a taxi straight to Bradford to score some crack cocaine.

In Bradford that night, having nowhere to stay, I made my way to an old friend's bedsit, got smashed and moved in. It was as simple as that. Tim and his girlfriend Sarah slept on one mattress, me on another and another bloke, Tom, slept on the floor. That same night Tim fell asleep wasted while his girlfriend was having sex with Tom. The next morning I woke up with her in my bed. When everyone else had woken up there was tension for a while but, after a few joints and pills, things were OK. Knowing it was only a matter of time before the cramps caught up with me, I tooled up as usual and went out to case the area, looking for somewhere to break in. I was back into my old routine. It would normally take me between one and three hours to find a house. Once I had made sure there was no one in, I would kick the door off its hinges or take a window out at the back and then search the house for electrical equipment, money, jewellery, antiques or anything valuable, piling it all up near the front door. I would never rush. If I did not have access to a car, I used to phone for a taxi, telling the driver I had fallen out with the wife and was taking my stuff back to my mother's. When the car arrived, I would load the car quickly in case the neighbours saw me. I would tell the taxi driver to take me to Bradford where I would sell the stuff and immediately buy a large weight of heroin and crack cocaine from dealers I knew. Then I would get another taxi back home to get wrecked. Back at the bed-sit the spoons and needles would already be out and the crack pipe already made. Sometimes the powder was stronger than others, depending on how close a friend the source was.

The next day Tim left the bed-sit never to return, which left Sarah and me alone. Never one to miss a money-making opportunity I came up with the idea that I could get her to work the street. That night I asked her if she was up for some fun and took her to a flat where I knew there would be people drinking, smoking pot and snorting powder. There were five lads there, all of whom I knew. I rolled joints and passed them round while Sarah had sex with all five of them. No one really cared who was doing what with whom. A few days later Sarah went missing with one of the guys.

I hadn't been out of prison long when I met up with Jenny again and we got back together. It was strange: we always ended up back together when one of us had been inside. It was like we needed something from each other, but we didn't know what. Our daughter Roxanne continued to live with Jenny's mum and dad. We celebrated the reunion but it was not long before reality struck and our money ran out. Then I was back out at night, climbing over rooftops, checking out alarms and weighing up jobs. The police were always sniffing around and people were getting busted regularly. I was always on my guard in case I was next. I did so many jobs that I knew I might be arrested at any time.

Living in an area where I had many enemies, I had to be on the lookout all the time. Sometimes I would bump into them in the street. You could deal with the enemies you knew about, but I seemed to have enemies I didn't even know, which was much more dangerous. One night I was in a top-floor flat chatting with a mate who happened to look out of the window and down the street where he saw a gang of about fifteen lads fanned out across the street, walking in the direction of the flat. They were obviously out to get someone and, having been told about a gang that was looking for me, I put two and two together. I had no weapons and I knew the lad I was visiting wasn't a fighter, so I had to move fast. I got out onto the fire escape at the back of the flats and tried to scramble down it as fast as I could, almost leaping from platform to platform instead of using the steps. I thought they might surround the building and since I had precious little time to get away I darted down to the basement area where there were a group of sheds side by side for residents to use.

There were nine sheds, only one of which I found was unlocked after quickly trying each one. I darted inside and wedged my back against the door with my feet against the wall. My heart was pounding. "What a stupid place to hide," I thought to myself. "If anything happened, no one would see or even hear." I heard some of the lads outside shouting to one another, "He couldn't have gone far. If I find him, I'm gonna kill him." I heard them begin checking the sheds, one by one, and gradually they were getting closer. I thought I was a dead man. I knew I didn't stand a chance against so many of them, but I was determined to go out fighting. They were about three sheds away from me when I heard a voice shout, "Leave it, he's not there. He must have gone round the other side, down by the river." Then they left. It was a close call. It took me a while to calm myself down. I had no idea who they were. I stayed where I was until I was sure they had gone. After that I made certain I always carried some sort of weapon with me. Sometimes I was the hunter, sometimes the hunted. It was a crazy lifestyle, but as far I could see, there was no way out – other than death. Things were getting on top of me. I had broken my prison licence yet again, I had lost count of how many jobs I had done since I got out, and my habit was mounting up.

I went to see a friend about a second-hand car. I knew he would let me have one on the usual basis of dropping in a bit of jewellery or cash now and again until it was paid off. Both of us knew that with a car I could move twice as many goods twice as fast. The car got me out of the area and it always came back full. With me risk never seemed to be an issue; neither did courage. I would park on someone's drive as if it was my own, break in and fill the car up, covering the goods with a blanket and always traded everything I stole for drugs.

Sometimes Jenny would come and load the car with me. As soon as we had sold all the stuff, we would go to a friend's to smoke and get wasted. One of the people we used to go and see quite a lot was a lunatic called Sam, who loved fighting. No matter what the situation was he would be behind you ready for action. His place was small but it was clean. After taking a hit, we used to play a game we had developed. It consisted of taking turns to throw a knife at one another's legs, but you weren't allowed to move your feet. We had some close calls but no one ever got injured.

After I had been out for a few months, things began to hot up. Some of my mates who had been arrested on suspicion and released told me that the police were always asking questions about where I was hanging out, so I knew they were on my case and would probably try and arrest me for something. I was on another downward spiral and the pressure was getting to me. The final straw came when I had a fight with two lads who had come looking for me at a dealer's house, trying to settle a debt. I was there when they arrived, but rather than confront them head on, I hid and waited for my moment. I laid low on the first floor waiting for them to come down. As they made their way down the final flight of stairs, I jumped on top of them and there was a very noisy struggle. I beat them off but I knew I'd had enough of this type of conflict. I needed to get out. I decided to go somewhere out of the area to chill until things cooled down a bit.

Taking about 250ml of Methadone with me to try and withdraw from heroin, I found a bed and breakfast place miles away in Huddersfield. But it was another half-hearted attempt which was bound to fail. After a few days I got to know some of the lads in the area who were injecting speed. In return for my Methadone, they gave me speed and we spent the next few days together, talking day and night and happily injecting one another. As always, when the gear started to run out, I began scanning the town for potential hits on shops, houses, factories, jewellers, bars, churches – there was no shortage of places. Physically and mentally I wasn't doing at all well. My body was trying to cope with all the stuff I was pumping into it and it was doing my head in. My body wanted heroin and I was pumping it full of speed. I needed more and more speed to take the edge off my craving. With no clean needles around I would re-use dirty ones, even ones with congealed blood on them. Sometimes they were so blunt they would bend before piercing the skin.

I had been in Huddersfield for about a month when I was arrested for handling stolen goods and using a replica weapon. I was released pending a court date. When the date came round I was given twelve months to attend a Drug Offender Support Programme. I agreed to attend but in reality I had no intention of doing so. It was a close shave, but I was still free. By now I was finding life in Huddersfield a bit dull so, spurred on by yet another fight, I decided to go back to my own area and the guys at home were pleased to see me back. Everything was the same. It was back to work as normal, planning jobs and dealing gear.

Back in Bradford, all you heard about was one violent attack after another. There was a lot of bloodshed. People were ganging together and, armed with machetes or guns, were kicking dealers' doors in and taking all their gear at knife or gun point. It was happening everywhere. For some it seemed the easiest way to get hold of drugs. One guy had a kettle full of boiling water poured over his bare feet to make him surrender his drugs. We were round a mate's house one night when two blokes had an argument and one of them pulled out a gun. Wherever we went, we went ready to deal with every eventuality. I would regularly go round with a baseball bat hidden under my clothes. I remember one day a couple of mates and I drove to a bloke's house to pick up some gear. For some reason they were expecting something to happen. As the bloke swung the door open he saw my baseball bat and quickly pulled out a knife. We quickly realized he also had backup and we knew we had to get out of there fast. There was no time to get back in the car, so we kept running. Behind us one of the blokes giving chase recognised our car and threw a fire extinguisher through the windscreen. We managed to get away but we were not about to let it end there.

Having skipped court and failed to surrender, I knew it was only a matter of time before the police caught up with me. I tried to lie low for a while, mainly burgling at night-time, but before long the inevitable happened: I was caught on a job and arrested. As usual the police held me for a few days, taking my shoes and jacket for forensics and questioning me about all sorts of jobs. I was charged, sent before the magistrate and in no time was back in Armley on remand. The prison doctor lived up to his reputation as "Dr No" and I found myself locked up in a cell with nothing to take the edge off my withdrawal. All that was left to me was to take my frustration out on my new cell mate. After months of waiting, I was sentenced to three and a half years and shipped to another prison. It was a long sentence.

On this stretch I spent as much time as I could in the gym, determined to get fit for the next time I was chased by the police. I also managed to get one of the prized jobs in the kitchens, where I concentrated a lot of my efforts on stealing fruit and yeast to make home brew to drink and sell to other inmates. We kept the brew in the roof where the sniffer dogs couldn't smell it out. Occasionally cells were searched and people busted, but it was all part of the game. Before I got nicked, I had been spending a lot of time with a bloke I met who was into dreams and tarot cards and was always trying to read our futures. The subject still fascinated me and I passed the long, lonely hours in my cell reading books on the supernatural, particularly on devils and witches. I was given a book called the *Necronomicon*, which should never have been in prison. It was all about demons with different powers and countless rituals, all of which required blood. I struck up a friendship with a bloke who had built an altar or shrine in his cell and kept a bowl of blood on it. He played loud heavy-metal music the whole time.

Towards the end of my three and a half years I decided that when I got out, I was going to move to another area and try and make a new start, try and break away from the lifestyle I was living. I was sick of my addictions, of going round and round in circles. I was really depressed, but no one else would have known. As far as everyone round about me was concerned I was still the happy-go-lucky guy I had always been. I always wore a mask to hide the real me, because I was afraid of the person underneath who wanted to change, who was always dreaming of what could have been ... I was still tormented by all my "if onlys". "If only I had done better at school ... If only I had got on with my family ... If only ... If only ... " Everyone I knew was either a psycho or a criminal or involved in the gang or drug scene. I desperately wanted to give myself a chance.

On release I decided I would move to Leeds and I was given some help to find a place. It was only about half an hour from my old area, but I managed to con myself that it was far enough away. After the usual pre-release treatment – in this prison it was being thrown into a cold bath fully clothed – I said my goodbyes and made my way to the Leeds Housing Office to pick up the keys for my new place. I finally found it in the middle of a run-down, graffiti-ridden estate. It was just one tatty, smelly room, but I had had worse. For the first few days I managed to keep away from my old friends, but that was mainly because on my new estate I bumped into loads of other people I had met on various prison stretches. On this estate it seemed even easier to get high and my resolve to change my lifestyle quickly crumbled. It wasn't what I had intended, but it seemed natural. High again, I soon went back to visit my old friends in Brooklyn. Nothing had changed, apart from the fact that they all looked a little bit the worse for wear. Their arms were like pin cushions: battered, bruised and pocked with abscesses. I had plenty of friends to visit, so it was several days before I went back to my place in Leeds.

I couldn't believe it when I found out that Jenny was in a bail hostel in Leeds, just thirty minutes' walk from where I was living. We met up and as usual we immediately got back together. She was still an addict and had just served a sentence in prison but, like me, she couldn't break free from the scene. Our crazy, violent relationship resumed where it had left off. We loved each other but somehow violence just seemed part of it. We would share whatever she acquired through shoplifting and sometimes we would go out shopping on other people's credit cards or forge people's signatures on their social security books to cash at post offices. All in all, within a few weeks of being released from prison, it was as if my life had never changed. Every single day I was out burgling or planning jobs with people in and out of the area, or selling stolen goods for people. There was always something to do that seemed urgent.

As well as my usual orders for gold, diamonds and electrical equipment, more and more people were asking for the wheels off high-performance sports cars. In prison I had met a guy who was a professional car thief and, knowing he was also out, I tracked him down and we met up. I wanted him to teach me the tricks of the trade. We hooked up together for the next few weeks, travelling the area and leaving a fair few cars on bricks with no wheels. Sometimes we would steal the car and use it to burgle houses. Once we had sold the equipment from the burglaries we would take the car to an isolated place and blow it up. As usual, all the proceeds went on drugs and drink. Once we had learnt what we both had to teach one another, we parted and went our separate ways.

The courts let Jenny off her charges – albeit with lots of conditions – and she managed to get a place back in our home town. I gave up my place in Leeds and joined her. It seemed we had gone full circle. After both having served a prison sentence we were back living together and dealing again. Occasionally we would go and see our daughter, but I was never allowed near the house. The family hated me with a vengeance. It used to really upset me but there was nothing I could do about it.

The drug and gang scene was worse than I had ever known it. All over the place there were turf wars going on, trying to establish who could sell what where, and if anyone was caught selling on someone else's patch they would not hesitate to smash their knee caps, cut them up, or even shoot them. People would do anything to make money and keep their own habits ticking over. If you couldn't handle yourself you were in the wrong game! One guy I knew had a very lucky escape. One night when he wasn't at home, a van drew up outside his house and ten men, all armed with baseball bats and wearing balaclavas, jumped out, kicked the front door down and smashed the whole place up, taking all the cannabis plants from his shed with them. People weren't messing around. We turned up at the house of another of our dealer friends to find her looking really shaken up. The night before she had been shot at in her own kitchen by two gunmen. To prove it, she showed me a huge bullet hole in the kitchen wall. They beat her up and took her gear and her car. I hated these situations. I knew exactly who had done it but I couldn't say anything; she was dealing on their patch and stealing their customers. They would have definitely shot her if she hadn't handed over the gear, so to come away with a few bruises was really a good result. Jenny comforted her and we cooked a hit together and then left.

I bumped into another old mate whom I'll call "T" when he was right in the middle of a situation. He was another real character and not the type of guy to be intimidated. Jenny and I went back to T and his girlfriend's place for an evening to score heroin and reminisce about old times in prison. You couldn't help notice the two-foot-long machete leaning against his fireplace. He was obviously expecting trouble. He told us that a crew of lads had been to his place a few days before, angry over some big deal that had gone wrong. To make sure he did a good job if they came back, we drove over to a friend's to borrow a sawn-off shotgun for a while. When the lads finally did come back, pulling out their tools as they walked down the path, they were welcomed by the twin barrels of the shotgun aiming at them through the letterbox. They never came back. T came on a few jobs with me as my driver, but he hated it. He was still on licence from prison for cutting someone up and that made him very jittery. T and his girlfriend broke up and I lost contact with him again.

Burgling no longer gave me the adrenalin buzz it used to. It was just a necessary part of my day – as natural as brushing your teeth. Nowadays I felt numb. Burgling during the day was always risky and I had a couple of close shaves. On one occasion, when our boot was full of stolen gear, the police chased me and a mate who was helping me. We hot-footed it to a gym another mate had just opened in the town. It was a genuine business – apart from the people snorting cocaine off the health bar surface and making crack cocaine with Bunsen burners. But the owner was pretty paranoid at the best of times – probably due to his own heavy use of coke – so he was always hearing noises and looking out for the police. We were just unloading our goods when he shouted "Police" and the whole place went mental. I had a gun on me and disappeared up on the roof to hide. To our relief they were just driving by checking things out and they drove off again almost immediately! After we had sold our gear and bought some crack we drove home and shared it with our women who had been withdrawing for hours.

Through the grapevine I heard again that the police were looking for me. It was only a matter of time. I had committed so much crime that I could never be certain exactly what they were after me for. A few weeks later at about 4.30 a.m. armed police kicked the front door off the flat and charged in. The whole street was swarming with cars, vans and dogs. I was arrested and dragged off to a police station miles away from my home. The next day I was interrogated about a local armed robbery at one of the post offices in my home town. I was kept in a few days and, as usual, questioned about a whole series of burglaries and car thefts in the area. The police told me they knew I was responsible for a lot of it and said I should watch my back because they were going to have me and, when they did, they would make sure I got slammed for a good few years. The way they were talking it seemed obvious that they had no evidence and sure enough, after a couple of days, I was released. I stole a car from the train station and headed home.

That night it was business as usual. But recent events and the fact that you constantly had to have your wits about you were taking their toll. I was becoming paranoid and very angry. It was as though I was caught up in some nightmare that would never end. I found that another gang was after me, this time over an antique ring I had stolen from someone they knew. They caught up with me a few days later back at our house. It was around teatime and it was still light outside. Three men wearing balaclavas and carrying axes ran up to our front door and began chopping it down. Jenny and I could see the blades coming through the door. There was no back door to the house and we were trapped. Two days before I had had a shotgun and a rifle in the house, but at that precise moment I had nothing. Thankfully, Jenny had her wits together and started shouting loudly, pretending to be calling the police. They heard the bogus call and ran off, vowing to be back. It was a narrow escape. I went to round up a few guys to back me up if they came back. Nothing could be done other than just to stay alert and watch my back.

A few days later, I was chatting with a mate at his flat when I noticed a car parked up outside. Discovering that it belonged to the guy upstairs, who was out at work, I broke into his flat, found his car keys and then loaded his car up with his TV, hifi and video. I was just driving the car off and about to turn left onto the main road when its owner, who was arriving back in another car, saw me and they gave chase. I swung out into the main road with them in pursuit. They had a much faster car and I wasn't able to put any distance between us, so, after a short chase, I abandoned the car and ran off. I wasn't caught that day but someone saw my face and recognised me. I was arrested a week later and interviewed over many days. I was charged and remanded into Armley prison to await sentencing. Sometimes when I was finally caught there was relief that I could rest for a while.

Chapter 7

Armley prison hadn't changed one bit. I knew I was going to have massive cold turkey. By the time I arrived I already had the cramps and was starting to sweat. There was no sleep that night. I was in serious pain, pacing up and down, alternating between being boiling hot and freezing cold and also hallucinating, but I managed to hold out until the morning.

On exercise I met up with my stepbrother Danny who had been in a week for a job on a jeweller's. He was also withdrawing and looked pretty bad. I asked him if he had anything to trade and, to my surprise, he still had a diamond ring on him that he had managed to hide. After much persuasion he trusted me to sell it and later that day it was sold for a large amount of powder. Trusted prisoners would have cleaning jobs and they were the ones who were in a position to slip the powder under the right person's cell door. Cold turkey was put off for a while.

The weeks soon turned into months. Every couple of weeks I would be taken to court to be remanded again to Armley prison. Knowing it would be years before I was released, my thoughts frequently turned to suicide, but this time I never gave in to it. Before I had just taken prison in my stride, but now it was beginning to really get to me. I knew it too well. I hated life. There was something inside me that was very sick and very angry. I wanted to smash the whole world to smithereens. I could see no way out and no way forward. Everyone was an enemy. But somehow I would survive. Finally, after around nine months, I was sent to Leeds Crown Court for sentencing. Handcuffed to two officers I was taken up to the court room. My charges and part of my criminal record were read out. For the umpteenth time I was told I was a menace to society and sentenced to three years and ten months. I thanked the judge; I was expecting at least five years.

Two months later I was sent back to the prison I had served my last sentence at, which was good as I knew my way around. It hardly seemed any time since I had left. There were plenty of drugs on offer, lots of wheeling and dealing behind the officers' backs, and a few fights in the showers for those who didn't pay their suppliers. But this time something in me was different. I was sick of it. All day long I would daydream about what could have been; what I would have been like without crime; what my family relationships would have been like without violence. I would get angry with myself for allowing such stupid thoughts to come into my mind and would cast them aside. It was too late. I had come too far. There was a battle going on inside of me. Part of me wanted to change; part of me didn't. I refused to acknowledge it and shut it all out, trying to forget all about it. I had a few years in here ahead of me and needed to pull myself together, big time. Change was for weak people and in prison they smell weakness a mile away.

Six weeks later my job came through and I was moved to the main part of the prison where I was given my own cell on a landing with thirteen others. I already knew a few guys on the corridor from my last sentence and was sorted out with the tobacco and gear I needed to take me through until pay day. It felt strange to be back with the same people I had left hardly any time ago, it seemed. But I treated prison merely as an occupational hazard. I started my job. It was OK and I made some good mates. Whenever I could, I trained hard at the gym. I took all my aggression out on the punch bag and most of the time I was buzzing.

A couple of the lads I had known for years started talking about a prison by the sea about 300 miles away. They said it ran a drug therapy programme and, most attractive of all, there were rumours that you had your own TV and a sea view! We laughed our socks off about it. I didn't know whether to believe it or treat it as a windup. One night I decided that the next morning, when the door was unlocked, I would go to the office to find out more about it. They gave me an address to write to but they said that because it was so far away, not many from our prison were accepted. Nevertheless, I walked away with the address. At this point I had no intention whatsoever of going for any "therapy"; I was looking for an easy ride for the rest of my sentence. I joked with my pals and told them I was going to go for it. We all found it hilarious. Little things please the mind when you're bored stupid. That night when I finally got back to my cell after a day of wheeling and dealing, I began to write to the Therapy Unit, pleading for help with my addiction. I wrote four sides of A4. It was a heart's cry, although to me it seemed I was half joking, half serious. The next day I posted the letter and forgot all about it.

The months passed slowly by, but finally one day I received a letter back from the Therapy Unit I had applied to. I couldn't believe it: they had accepted me! The Unit was located in HMP Channings Wood in Newton Abbot, Devon, and the letter said that arrangements were being made to transport me there sometime soon. "Soon" turned out to be very soon and a month or so later I was on a prison coach, handcuffed to a mate, both excited about our destination. That evening, when we stopped at another prison for the night before carrying on the next day, I realized just how much distance we had covered. It meant there would be no chance of visits from anyone – not that I had been getting any lately, but the possibilities were now absolutely zero.

The following day, as the roads turned into country lanes and the prison finally came into view, I began to wonder if I had been conned. For a start, there was no sign of any sea, and the prison looked the same as every other one I had been to: high walls, gloomy, old-fashioned, covered with bars and razor wire. What had I let myself in for? Coming off the coach we were greeted with a smile from some pretty friendly officers. This was unusual and made me wonder why they were being so soft. I felt uncomfortable; I wasn't used to nice screws. They uncuffed us all and took us to reception to be kitted out and given the usual induction talk. I found out that most of the guys in the main prison didn't like the people on the Therapy Community (TC), where I was going, because they got little perks and ran it themselves. This made no sense to me. I couldn't see how the TC could be in the prison and yet separate from it at the same time; and the idea that the prisoners ran it themselves seemed difficult to believe. An officer appeared from the Unit. He was smiling and welcoming. "What is it with all these happy people?" I wondered to myself. "They're making me sick. If he's so happy, why doesn't he just let us all go and we'll promise that we'll never do it again!"

Carrying our bed rolls we went through a few gates that were locked behind us before we finally arrived at the Unit itself. There were quite a few cons about. They were all wearing shirts that had brightly coloured badges on. The first thing I noticed was that they all had the same stupid smile I had been greeted with at the gate, like they were having a silly-grin competition or something. We were taken into the office to be introduced to some of the staff. To my surprise they wore their own clothes. To my even greater surprise some were ex-addicts. I was introduced to the two "co-ordinators" of the community, who were two prisoners serving time. Apparently, towards the end of the programme, the prison staff overseeing the programme took a back seat and let two co-ordinators take a leading role. It was too much. I couldn't get my head round it. And to make things worse, when I got to my cell there was no TV and no sea view!

Later that evening I was taken to the office and asked to sign a contract to say I would be willing to change and abide by the rules. I signed it begrudgingly. After that I met a few guys from the Bradford area who had been in the Unit a long time. By now I was feeling totally confused about the place. I had already had an interview with my personal officer and told her, for a joke, that I fantasised about chopping people up and eating them. When I told my old mates what I'd said they didn't react in the way they normally would have done. They had changed somehow and didn't think it was funny. As we talked, they filled me in on the place. They called it a "self-help community". It meant that if there was a problem with a person's behaviour or attitude, the other people in the community (cons and staff) would point it out to them. If they took it well, fine. But if they took it negatively they were taken to a group "encounter" later in the week, at which people challenged them on their behaviour. If they accepted what they were told without demonstrating any further bad attitude, they got off with a warning which was logged in "the book" – a kind of journal detailing the misdemeanours of everyone in the Unit. To me it was totally bizarre. My mates had changed so much.

That same evening I had to attend a meeting run by prisoners. There were about eighty men there with the two co-ordinators at the front. It was mental: they introduced me and welcomed me into the community, and then the whole room started clapping. I found it totally embarrassing. I was sure I was at the funny farm and somehow I had been brought here by mistake. In the same meeting people were called out to the front and given different badges, which meant they moved on to a deeper level of recovery and were given more responsibility. That evening, alone in my cell, I thought of ways of trying to get back up north. I wasn't sure I wanted to change. Who was to say whether I was ready or not? I was starting to think I was in a place full of lunatics and that even my mates from home had been completely brainwashed.

But gradually I found myself getting used to the place. Over the next few weeks I made some good friends who seemed different from all the friends I had ever had before in a way that I couldn't explain. The staff were OK once you got used to them. But I was constantly being told off by the other prisoners about my attitude and my aggressive behaviour, so two weeks running I found myself taken to task in the encounter group. Did I have an attitude? You bet I did. Basically my whole attitude to the community was that they were all wrong and I was right! I was very aggressive towards people and often swore at members of staff and inmates. I was constantly disrespectful and didn't observe the rules of the community: i.e. not shaving, walking on wet floors, keeping my cell untidy on purpose and just rebelling in general. After a number of such instances I found myself with a final warning: if I didn't shape up, I would be out. I was called to the main office and given an ultimatum. I was told I would be on the next coach back up to Yorkshire if I didn't accept change and if they didn't see an improvement in my behaviour. I realized that they meant what they said and decided I would give it a go. One of the things that struck me about this community was that you had to write your whole life story down on a piece of paper and meet in groups where you would stand at the front and read it out. It was a really big deal for all of us to be vulnerable like that because we had all spent most of our lives trying to hide our pain behind bravado. What struck me was that many people's stories were very similar to mine. At this point I realized that it wasn't just me who had had a rough deal in the world and I began to chill out and accept change because I understood I wasn't alone with my pain and anger. Each day the whole community gathered in a room in the morning and again in the evening and the philosophy and rules that we were to live by were read out. I can't recall all of what was said, but one concept for living really stuck in my mind and helped me begin to change. It was, "Act as if and you will become as if". They claimed that if you really believed change was possible and began to act as if you had changed, then eventually you would discover that you had changed.

Change took a while but people were very patient with me. As the months went by, I began to feel different and I gradually began to get serious about change. I learnt all the rules of the community off by heart and then moved on to the concepts they gave us to live by. Although it was hard, I enjoyed the process of change. For the first time in my life – apart from the responsibility of my children which I had not made a good job of – I was given some proper responsibility. In no time two years had passed and I was still there. I had gone a whole two years without taking drugs. It felt strange, but good; in fact, it felt amazing. I would never have believed that I could make it so far. Then I was even offered the job of a co-ordinator of the community, which I accepted. It was the first time in my life I had ever achieved something! I was on a high and became passionate about seeing people through their recovery. If it could happen to me, it could happen to anyone.

As a co-ordinator of the community I would meet with the other co-ordinator and staff members each morning to discuss the day and the progress of different individuals in the community. The co-ordinators would take the morning and evening meetings, delegate work, carry out job appraisals and organise personal reports about people's progress and change. We also organised inductions for new people and sat in on encounters to make sure everything was going smoothly and that the correct rules and tools were being applied. Each week I would meet new people for induction coming from other prisons. The moment they walked through the gate onto the Unit I could see the same anger and confusion I had experienced: "Why is everyone smiling? How come the place is so clean?" But now I knew that the course worked and no matter how ugly, how big, how tattooed or how angry the person looked, if it could work for me it could work for them. I became totally immersed in the programme because of my passion to see others change. I've always been an "all or nothing" type of person, so once I realized the system worked I gave it my all.

Over the two years I made some good friends. One very close friend was Matthew. He was OK, even though he was one of the God squad and always banging on about Jesus and going to church. He had a little cross in his cell and a Bible on his table. I would sometimes wind him up about his faith, but it never seemed to bother him. Matthew was from Manchester and as soon as we met we got on great. He was a backslidden Christian who had committed some crimes when he got involved with drugs and was sentenced for it. Matt was always talking to me about Jesus. He had a good sense of humour and would often laugh like a hyena. He was a chunky, well-built guy and he reminded me of Popeye! Even though I wasn't a Christian and didn't understand what on earth he was doing he would lie on his bottom bunk at night with me above him on the top bunk, and pray for me in a funny language. I couldn't look him in the face whenever he did it because it made me laugh – it sounded so weird! But I knew in his own way he was trying to help so I let him get on with it.

One Sunday he asked me to go along to church with him. I thought about it. What did I have to lose? I think the thing that did it was that he told me there was tea and chocolate biscuits after the service. Chocolate biscuits were like gold in prison. Anyway, at least it would kill a bit of time, so I agreed. That evening the lads came to get me for chapel and off we went. Churches always gave me the creeps. At the door the Prison Chaplin, Martin, greeted us all with a firm handshake. He introduced himself and we had a brief chat. Then things got going. We sang a few strange songs and the preacher

this by His teaching, by healing the sick, by raising people from the dead and by casting out demons from those who were possessed. Then, though His death, He showed us that He loved us so much that He was willing to be nailed to the cross to take the sins of the world on His shoulders, and that included mine. Martin's voice was full of excitement as he got to the best bit of the good news and explained that Jesus hadn't just died on the cross and that was the end of it, but having been buried in a stone tomb, on the third day He had risen from the dead in victory and He is now seated on a throne in Heaven by the side of God the Father. The whole reason Jesus did all this was so that I could have a relationship with God today. Getting even more animated Martin explained that because of what Jesus had done, my past could be dealt with. For years I had been called "Jaffa" as a nickname and Martin kept shouting, "Down with Jaffa, up with Mark!" I was absolutely blown away by what I was hearing. It was a lot to take in. I needed to think. As our meeting came to an end, Martin gave me a piece of paper with a prayer written on it, which a person could pray if they wanted to receive Jesus into their heart and life.

Meeting with Martin and hearing all about Jesus had stirred something up within me which I couldn't understand and I definitely couldn't explain. Back on the Unit I tried to go about my tasks for the rest of the day. Eventually the day came to an end and I was relieved to be locked in my cell for the night; peace at last. I waited for every other door to be locked and listened as the keys began to jingle off into the distance. As I slowly began to wind down, I thought about Jesus. I started thinking about all the movies I had seen in which there was a battle between good and evil and the good always won. I realized that for many years I myself had been caught up in a battle between good and evil, between God and the devil. I had been deceived. I had only ever known the devil, hatred, jealousy, violence, greed. I felt tearful. I was overwhelmed. I can't explain why. Thinking more deeply about my battle I realized it had been against Jesus; it had been against love, joy and peace. I thought about what I had been told. I closed my eyes and pictured Jesus hanging on the cross for me. I got off my bed and knelt on the floor of my cell and prayed. I asked God to forgive me for all the sin in my life and said that I needed Jesus to help me change. Then I thanked Jesus for dying for me on the cross and asked Him to come into my life. I didn't know what to expect. There was certainly no thunder or flashes of lightning. I was very tired and crawled into bed.

The next morning, as soon as I opened my eyes, I knew something had changed. For one thing I had never slept so well. I jumped out of bed, feeling free and happy. It felt like a weight had been lifted off me. I felt like singing and dancing. That morning as I opened the curtains, I was greeted with a beautiful day. As I looked around at the trees and birds and flowers, I realized that for the first time I could really see their beauty. Through the window I could smell all sorts of perfumes that I had never even noticed before. I was fascinated by my new knowledge that God had made them. The thought that God was now my Father made me smile even more. As Martin had explained to me, the Bible says, *"you will know the truth, and the truth will set you free"* (John 8:32), and I felt really free.

Soon afterwards, the cell door opened and the day started. During the day I told a few people that I had given my life to Jesus. Given my background as a joker, not many believed me at first. Most people thought I had finally lost the plot and gone away with the fairies! Over the next few days I could feel I was already growing stronger. I had surprised myself. I knew in my heart I was free and I decided to take a stand. My opportunity came at my next meeting as co-ordinator. In front of fifty men I stood up and said that I had now given my life to Jesus Christ and that if anyone ever called me "Jaffa" again they would have to account for it to an encounter group. I told them, " 'Jaffa' was my old name. From now on it's Mark. Jaffa is dead!" After the meeting I saw my new Christian brothers who had taken me to church buzzing with excitement and encouraging me to go for it. Others shook my hand and I was able to share the little I knew with them. A few days later, at chapel, I got the chance to tell Martin the good news. When I told him I had said the prayer, we rejoiced together. Then he gave me a pocket-sized Gideon's Bible and explained to me how to read it. Just before I left, Martin told me there was a job going in the prison chapel and that I should pray about it. Too right I would!

When I got back on the Therapy Unit everything was pretty quiet as everyone was in meetings. I put the Bible in my cell, excited at the prospect of reading it that evening and got on with the rest of the day. I went to the main office for an application form for the chapel job and filled it out. It was time I moved on. I only had two weeks left in therapy, then I would have to get another job off the wing. If I got the chapel job, it would be absolutely perfect timing.

That evening, after the usual mad, last-minute rush of everyone running round swapping magazines and papers to read for the night and making cups of tea, the doors were all locked and I was finally alone. The moment I had been looking forward to had come. I opened my new Bible and tried to start reading it, but immediately something happened inside my head and I started blaspheming and shouting all sorts of obscenities against God. A voice inside my head was saying, "It's all lies, it's all just rubbish." But then, all of a sudden, an audible shout came from my own mouth, "You can't say that, Mark." I had no idea where it came from. It couldn't have been me, could it? I didn't understand it; it didn't make sense. I sat on my bed and wondered if my neighbours in the cells above and either side had heard me shout out. I looked across at my Bible. I was quite scared at what had just happened. I began to analyse the words carefully, *"You can't say that, Mark."* It was a statement. It wasn't me talking. When I realized it was God, I was relieved and amazed. A feeling of peace came over me and once again I got off my bed and sat at the table to read the Bible. I opened it at the very beginning where there was a list of topics with Scripture references under each one. On the left-hand side of the page, at the very top, the first thing I read was my own name "Mark" and, underneath it, the word "afraid", with some other words like "bereaved", "broken-hearted" and "depressed". Right by "afraid" was the reference Mark 5:1. When I looked it up, I found it was a story about a violent man who was possessed by an evil spirit. He was so strong and so dangerous that the local villagers had to chain him up, but he would often smash off his shackles and start roaming around the neighbourhood. One day, however, Jesus arrived in the locality by boat and immediately the possessed man ran up to him. Jesus was able to cast the demons out of the man, sending them into a herd of pigs which were grazing nearby, causing them to rush headlong off the cliff and drown in the sea. For the first time in years the man was restored to his right mind. This was my first experience of reading the Word of God and I was just amazed at how relevant this story was to my life. I couldn't wait to read more. I began to realize that the Bible was not just a book but that it was living and powerful. I was hungry for more.

By now the guys on the landing knew the change in me was for real. I had joined the God squad full on and I wasn't ashamed of the Gospel of Jesus Christ. When no one was around, some of the lads would come into my cell, push the door to behind them and ask for prayers for their children or other members of their family. Often I hadn't a clue what I should pray for them and God would just put words in my mouth. I would pray things for them and words would come out that I never expected to say. It took a long time for people on the Unit to accept that I had a real faith and hadn't lost the plot. But when they realized I was genuine and was willing to stand up for what I believed, they began to trust me and many more came to talk to me and have me pray for them. The first time it happened it just felt normal and right. I almost expected it.

I really wanted the job in the prison chapel but I heard that there were a lot of other people interested and there was a waiting list. I began to pray and cry out to God in secret that I would get the job. I began to search the Bible for scriptures and found one in John 14:13 that says, *"I will do whatever you ask in my name, so that the Son may bring glory to the Father."* After a few weeks I was overjoyed to hear that I had got the prison chapel job and began work immediately. It was such an exciting time and God was doing so much in my life that I almost forgot I was in prison! I was growing as a Christian and learning fast all the time.

God was really on the move in my life. I would often fall asleep with my head in my Bible, I was so hungry for the Word. I would hang on every word that I read. My job in the chapel was perfect because it meant I had the opportunity to be off the wing and in a quiet place to pray. I would clean the toilets and keep the chapel tidy, and I would get the place ready for many different types of service since it was a multi-faith building. During the day after my chores I would watch Alpha videos and read my Bible. The sex offenders unit which was segregated from the rest of the prison would also have a special service there. These people were hated by the rest of the prison community, so anything they did had to be done separately. I would often sit in with these men, however, and sing hymns along with them because I believed God could heal them and I figured it was what Jesus would have done. Just six months prior to this, if I'd had the chance to be alone with those guys I would have gone in armed with a razor blade and looked to cut one of them up. I was coming to realize that only God can change people's hearts and what was so exciting was that he was changing mine. I was consumed with the Gospel. Often I would be ridiculed for sitting in this service, but that was OK because the Bible said things aren't always easy for followers of Jesus.

Through my work in the prison chapel I met another chaplain called the Rev. Bill Hill. He was an amazing man. He really loved the prisoners, regardless of what they were in for and, despite the fact that he wouldn't stand for any messing about, had won the respect of everyone, whether they were Christians or not. He had got hold of some guitars which he would lend out to inmates during their stay. When people wanted to be baptised, since there was no pool, he would baptise them in a dustbin. The person would get in the dustbin as a sign of cleansing the trash from their life, and then the water was tipped away. I developed a great friendship with Bill. I didn't know it then, but later when I was released from prison I would meet up with Bill again and he would help me grow in my faith.

When I made the decision to get baptised, realizing it was something commanded in the Bible, it was actually a minister called Martin Kiddle who baptised me and he managed to get the prison governor's permission to have a blow-up paddling pool brought to the chapel. I had escaped the dustbin (praise God)! I thought only a few would come to the service from the Therapy Unit, but on the day around thirty men and staff filled the small chapel. It was an awesome day. The presence of God filled the place and touched other lives. Matthew decided to rededicate himself publicly to God that day, in the same water I was baptised in. Tragically, when he was eventually released he fell back into the world of drugs, began to use again and I heard that he had overdosed and died. My friend, Matthew, who had first invited me to church where I committed my life to Christ. What a waste.

The months rolled by quickly and, through Alpha and other courses the chaplaincy ran, I was growing in my faith all the time. I saw many others give their hearts to God and get baptised. Just like me, their lives were changed as they trusted the Lord Jesus Christ and His power to heal and restore their lives. Finally my time in prison was coming to an end. I was so caught up in the great things that were happening that my release date was already in sight by the time I remembered I had nowhere to go when I was released from jail. I knew I couldn't go back to my old area – it would be like swimming with crocodiles. Everyone I had ever known was mixed up in the underworld; they were either criminals or psychos; quite a lot of them were both. I knew I had to pray earnestly and in my cell I prayed many times for God to make a way where there didn't seem to be any way. My prayers focused on three things: I needed to move somewhere well away from my old drugs and crime turf so I could truly make a fresh start; I prayed that I would find a job; and I prayed that I would find a wife. I wanted a fresh start, a clean break in a new area, and I believed for it with all my heart.

Chapter 8

God heard my prayers and answered them in remarkable ways. I still find it hard to believe how God orchestrated every little detail. He is awesome! A little time before I was due to be released, a couple called Ted and Mary Sandford, from a tiny village in Devon, had been coming into the prison on Tuesday nights to do a Bible study with us. We became great friends. After the meetings we would chat and pray for one another. I told them about my situation and asked if they would pray for me during the week while they were at home. They agreed. But without my knowing they contacted the prison governor and asked if I could go and stay with them for a while when I got out. Ted was a minister and ran an Anglican church in his village. The Governor agreed to the plan and two days before Christmas Eve I was released with a big smile on my face and a few possessions in a brown bag to go and start a new life in Devon. The faithfulness of God is amazing! I was discovering that what the Bible says is true:

> *"Trust in the LORD with all your heart*
> *and lean not on your own understanding;*

in all your ways acknowledge him,
and he will make your paths straight."

(Proverbs 3:5–6)

I was glad to be far away from the criminal underworld I had been immersed in for so long. Though I missed Jenny and Roxanne and wondered how they were doing, I knew that now was not the right time to go back and try to see them. I had written one letter to Jenny at the beginning of my time in the Therapy Unit to tell her I was changing for real. The response I'd received hadn't been very nice and we didn't speak to one another again for a long time. I never found out what her reaction was to the news that I'd become a Christian. To this day I'm not sure what is going on in her life, but I do know that she has another child and is happy. But regardless of Jenny's reaction to my change of direction, I had to be realistic. I had only just walked out of prison and I knew that if I travelled back to Yorkshire and began meeting up with all my old friends and associates I wouldn't last long; the pull of my old lifestyle and old habits would be too much to bear. All my friends were criminals and druggies – every one of them! And I knew the Bible spoke about the fact that I had become a new creation; old things had passed away and everything was made new. For now, that meant being a new person in a new area with no ties to my old way of living.

My new home was set deep in the Devon countryside, surrounded by rolling hills as far as the eye could see. It was an old rectory with huge grounds. Each morning I would meet with Ted and Mary, pray, and thank God for His goodness and mercy. It was Christmastime – a time that suddenly took on new and profound meaning for me. After the Christmas celebrations I set to work chopping down trees with a huge axe and mending fences. It felt amazing. It was enjoyable chopping logs, doing some physical exercise to burn off my excess energy, with the blood pumping through my veins and the smell of the country air. Each day there would be so much to do. But, at the same time, these first few months were the hardest to endure of my "new start". I didn't know my way around the area, so I was basically stuck in the middle of nowhere. On many occasions I was tempted to disappear off and find a drink or some drugs to smoke. But now at least I understood that, even though the temptations were strong, to give in to them would destroy the process of change I had gone through. I knew it would damage my faith and I didn't want that. I also had to fight the temptation to go out and find a woman to have sex with – which was the "manly" thing every con did when he was released; it was part of the ritual of being inside and then coming out. I found this really difficult, but the devil didn't beat me and I stood firm in God.

After about a month I found my way down into the local village and located a bus stop where I could catch a bus into Exeter. I wanted to look up Bill Hill, my old prison chaplain, who had often spoken about his church in the centre of Exeter. I had promised him I would check it out as soon as I could. I found the place, but "Riverside Church" looked nothing like a church to me! I met Bill and we rejoiced at seeing each other for the first time outside of prison. Bill showed me around the massive building which had fifty rooms in all, including a café, youth rooms, conference rooms and offices. I had never seen anything like it and it certainly didn't fit my perception of what a church should look like. It had previously been a night club and the church had bought it and converted it. John Partington was the pastor. Under his leadership the church was thriving and it became so packed on a Sunday that they had to run three services to get everyone in who wanted to come.

I began attending the church and was thrilled to find myself in a vibrant Christian community. But, amazingly, even amongst Christians I would be challenged and tempted. Exeter is a city with its drug problems just like any other and there were some ex-druggies that had become Christians who attended the church. At least, I assumed they were *ex*-druggies. For a short while I hung around with some of them until one day I was offered cannabis and sex by a woman at the church. I recognised the danger signs and withdrew immediately. I didn't miss the violence or the drugs or the crime that characterised my former life, but the most difficult thing I encountered in my Christian walk was people, like this woman, who lived a compromised lifestyle. They were neither black nor white, hot nor cold, and I didn't like it. It irritated me that many Christians I met were wimps and not warriors! The Bible says we are soldiers of the Cross. I loved chatting to other Christians, but I found a few of them could be extremely boring. Somewhat harshly I labelled them the "socks and sandals brigade"!

Bill and I met regularly for chats and our friendship grew strong. There was always work that needed to be done around the church so I agreed to come and do some voluntary painting, starting on two small rooms in the building. Three weeks later I was still there painting! I had painted several massive corridors and several different rooms. At weekends I loved attending the services where people would dance, raise their hands in the air and generally have fun and smile. John Partington would preach the Word of God and I liked his down to earth, practical style. His messages were scratching where I was itching and I loved his irrepressible enthusiasm for Jesus.

Getting to church on a Sunday wasn't always easy from the countryside where I was based. I did sometimes get a lift from members of the church, but that wasn't always possible. Then one Monday morning, as I was getting ready for another painting session at the church, came a real breakthrough. John came to see me for a chat and asked me how I was. Before I'd managed to reply to him he was already saying, "Come with me" as if there was something on his mind. He took me to some huge rooms located behind the main stage in the church's meeting hall, which were full of old boxes and cobwebs. He just came straight out with what he was thinking: "Why don't we build you a flat here? We'll make a bedroom, plumb a cooker in, put in some radiators, buff the floor . . . " I couldn't believe what he was saying. God was so gracious to me. I was overjoyed. I accepted John's offer and almost straight away I set to work. Bill offered to help me and together we built the flat. A few months later when it was ready, God answered the second prayer I had prayed regarding my new start – that I would find a decent job. When I finally moved into the flat it was as church caretaker and security guard – a servant in the house of God. I was so grateful to God and grateful to John for believing in me. John and his wife Andrene were to become great friends in my life.

During my time at the rectory I had had plenty of opportunity to think about my life and all the damage I had done to others. Although there was little I could do about making restitution to the hundreds of people I'd ripped off or hurt over the years, I felt God direct me to contact a few people. I began to pray and write letters to my mother, asking for forgiveness for how I had lived, and to my children. Ted helped me write them and we prayed over them before sending them, giving the rectory's address for people to reply to. I asked each of my kids for forgiveness for the way I had lived and the way in which I had neglected them. The first letter was sent to the youngest of my daughters who was living with her grandmother. The initial response came via a private phone call to the vicar from the girl's grandmother, warning him that he had a vicious thug living with him and to get out of the house immediately. Ted explained that I was no longer the same person who used to do all those things and suggested they should leave it a couple of months and then get in touch to see how I was doing. By the time they got in touch again I was living and working in Exeter. A date was arranged when they would come down and meet with me. Needless to say it was a hugely emotional but happy event. I asked my daughter to forgive me and she did. We have been friends ever since and our relationship has grown stronger.

Then something amazing happened. My eldest daughter tracked me down and sent me a letter asking if we could meet. This was the daughter I didn't "officially" know I had. At the beginning of chapter 3 I briefly described the first serious relationship I'd had with a girl whilst I was still in my teens and living with my gran. The girl became pregnant but she insisted that the baby was not mine and went off with another man. She gave birth to a girl, but this girl was, in reality, my daughter. I was shocked to receive this news some sixteen years later. I was curious, excited, but also extremely nervous. We arranged to meet and I travelled to Yorkshire to see her. There was no doubt about it, she was my own flesh and blood. Again, I asked her for forgiveness and we have a good relationship now. Contact with my third daughter, Roxanne, was arranged by my mother. We met at Mum's house and she also was willing to forgive me. One by one, God had restored my relationships with my daughters. It was totally amazing.

God also mended my broken relationship with my mum. Our first meeting after years of being estranged from one another happened at her house. We had a great day together. I asked her for forgiveness and she gave it. She couldn't believe the change in me. It was then that I discovered a twist in my mum's story. I had had no idea about the events that had taken place in her life because of being away in prison and having zero contact with her. Tired of the years of abuse and alcoholism she had run away with a man who lived with his family next door but one to her and Allan. In the middle of the night they quietly packed their bags and ran away together with no explanation, both leaving large families behind. They had moved to Blackpool and eventually, after a long time, came back and got married. Obviously there was a lot of anger about their relationship from their respective families and, true to form for our family, there was literally a fight in the aisle on their wedding day! But now Mum is happy, I have a relationship with her again, and it is probably the best thing that has ever happened to her. Sadly I have never been reconciled with my father.

During one of my visits back to Yorkshire the police found out I had been in the area and were also presented with the news that I had changed and become a Christian. It must have been hard to believe at first, I'm sure, but after a while one CID officer, Nick Greenwood – a policeman who had been my arch-enemy and had chased me all over Yorkshire – tracked me down. I received a text message from him saying that he had heard about what had happened and would like me to come and speak to a group of young offenders. I was very nervous about getting in touch with him; it felt like my past crimes were waiting to catch up with me! But I eventually called him and arranged a time to go with him to speak to a group of young lads. Coming face to face with the law, but on completely different terms than before, was a nerve-wracking experience. All the time my mind was telling me, "It's a set up. You'll be arrested!" We met, however, and I gave the talk and it went well. Afterwards Nick asked me where I'd received all my training to speak to large groups of people, because he was amazed at my self-confidence and ability to hold the group's attention. After many occasions where, across a police interview table, I had lied through my teeth to this man, for once I was able to tell him the truth: I had no training in public speaking and it was God who gave me the ability. After that Nick and I became friends and we still keep in touch. What had seemed impossible had become possible with God!

Meanwhile it was a privilege to sit under John Partington's inspirational teaching and grow as a Christian. As the church caretaker I was able to sit in on many of the meetings and conferences that took place in the building. After I had been a part of Riverside Church for about a year they decided to start running a Bible school called the "School of Acts". It would provide people with solid biblical teaching and hands-on experience in evangelism, praying for the sick and serving others. I knew it was the perfect next step for me and I wanted to go on the course, but I had a problem – there was a fee which, to me, represented a large sum of money and there was no way I could afford it. Taking a step of faith I asked God for a miracle. I prayed that if He wanted me to attend the Bible school He would open a way for me to do so. The very same day two widows who attended the church stopped me and asked if they could sponsor me to do the course. Every month without fail a cheque or cash came in to pay my school fees as

I sat under the teaching of Charlie Ross, the Dean of the School of Acts. During the School I had the chance to go on a mission to Portugal. John Partington went and we conducted street evangelism with the help of interpreters. On one occasion John and I were walking through a park when we were approached by a group of teenage girls. I was wearing shorts and a T-shirt so they could see the tattoos covering my body. They assumed that I was a drug dealer and stopped us to see if they could buy drugs from me. I told them, "I don't have drugs any more, but I do have Jesus!" John and I sat down with them and we ended up leading them to Christ. Through events like these my faith grew stronger and stronger; I had never been so free.

Now I turned my attention to the third and last prayer request on my list. In prison I had always dreamed of having a proper family; of settling down and living a normal life. Before I was released I had asked God for a wife; now I began to pray for one in earnest. I was specific in my prayers and I asked God for a woman who would love Him with a fiery heart and put Him before me. I didn't care what she looked like as long as she loved Jesus! Because of that prayer I met the most beautiful woman. God has blessed me with a wonderful wife in Andrea and we now have a baby son, Charlie.

The events leading up to our marriage had God's finger-prints all over them. Living and working in the church I constantly met new people. Being very different from most of the lads who attended the church with my Yorkshire accent and numerous tattoos, I found that I had gathered a few "fans" amongst the girls of the church, though I was very careful about how I handled these friendships. I only wanted what God wanted for me in terms of a serious relationship. One group of three girls was particularly friendly and since they lived together just two streets away from the church they would constantly invite me round for coffee and offer the use of their computer for me to check my emails. I often popped round there since it gave me a break from being in the church 24–7. One summer the girls were attending the New Wine Bible week in Shepton Mallet when they got chatting to another girl they'd just met. It was Andrea. Andrea had just completed a doctorate in clinical psychology (God has a sense of humour!) and was thinking about where to base herself to look for work. It's difficult for either of us to explain what happened looking back now – it was just one of those God-things – but Andrea felt God tell her to move to Exeter and share a house with these girls. All of them agreed that it felt right and so that's what she did.

It wasn't long until I met Andrea on one of my regular visits for coffee. There was something about her that was different and I think God planted the seed of things to come at that point. I went back frequently to "check my emails" even though I hardly ever received an email, just so I could see and talk to Andrea! Gradually we became good friends and spent a bit more time together. After a few weeks Andrea received the offer of a job in Glastonbury. She was debating whether to take the job and wanted to work out how feasible it was to make a daily commute there from Exeter. She asked me if I would drive there and back with her and time the journey and I agreed. It proved to be a life-changing trip! We stopped at a popular tourist spot in Glastonbury and sat together on the grass on top of a hill surrounded by beautiful scenery. Andrea shocked me by telling me, "God has given me an over-whelming love for you." It freaked me out and I responded by telling her, "Well, He hasn't said anything to me about it!" But we agreed to go away and pray about it. Back in Exeter we gave each other some space for a while and I prayed earnestly about whether she was the woman God had prepared for me. God graciously gave us both confirmation by independently showing us the same scripture indicating the rightness of our relationship. To be doubly sure, we went off and prayed again for a few more weeks and God again confirmed by His Word that we were meant to be together. In retrospect this time was more about me being sure about our relationship than Andrea. She had already secretly told her father that I was the man she would marry. Andrea had read a book by David Yonggi Cho in which he advises people to be very specific in their prayers and to write them down. So she had written out a detailed description of what her husband-to-be would be like. She even thought to specify the colour of his eyes, but here she had a bit of difficulty. She couldn't decide whether she wanted her husband to have blue eyes or green eyes. When she met me she discovered I had both – I have one blue eye and one green eye! So I guess God answered her prayer very thoroughly.

After that we began dating in earnest and I made up my mind to propose to her. Never one to do things by halves I came up with a crazy scheme to ask her to marry me. A friend of mine owned a horse. My plan, if you can believe it, was to hire a knight's costume from the local fancy dress shop and actually ride into the church hall during a meeting – her knight in shining armour! Unfortunately or fortunately perhaps, depending on your viewpoint, the horse wasn't available when I needed it, and so I found myself at the fancy dress shop selecting an alternative outfit. The only costume that would completely disguise me and deliver the desired surprise to Andrea was a Sylvester the Cat outfit! I hired it and hid it away in the back of the church. The occasion where I would propose was the Christmas Eve service at Riverside. John Partington was in on the scheme and at the appropriate point in the service he gave me a wink. I told Andrea I was popping to the toilet and slipped out of the service. A couple of minutes later John announced that it was time to welcome a "special visitor" and I came out dressed as Sylvester. John called Andrea up to the front of the church and I took the costume head off and proposed to her in front of the whole church. She said yes!

Our wedding was a time of great blessing and an occasion to give thanks to God for His overwhelming goodness and provision. On the big day, waiting as the music quietened I turned to look down the aisle at the most beautiful woman I had ever seen, and sensed the beginning of many new adventures. So many people from the church blessed us in so many ways. The wedding cake was provided as a free gift. The venue was provided free of charge and the band played for free. Many of our friends in the church served as waiters and waitresses at the reception. It was all quite overwhelming. For our honeymoon we were able to go to Cancun in Mexico. Andrea and I had dreamed of being able to swim together with dolphins, but knew it was an excursion that would be too expensive and extravagant for us. But after receiving around forty different envelopes from friends in the church, all containing gifts of money, we had enough money to swim with the dolphins. It was an extraordinary experience; something I would never previously have thought I would ever do.

Soon after we were married Andrea accompanied me on several visits back up to Yorkshire. Whilst we were travelling around I never saw any of my old mates – apart from one. We were stopped at some traffic lights when an old friend spotted me in the car and came over. As soon as he opened his mouth I could tell he was totally off his face. He asked me if I could lend him a fiver. Andrea found it hilarious that a guy who I'd not see for years could come straight up to me in the street and say, "Hi Mark, can you lend me five quid?" We visited various different members of my family and their response to my having become a Christian was usually one of bewilderment and amazement. My gran had died by this time, but my Auntie Cheryl was pleased to see what had happened in my life. She said it was "about time I grew up". That was how she saw it. My brother Danny, in particular, just couldn't believe I was the same person he'd known for all those years. When Andrea and I visited him, for whole duration of the meeting he sat there with his mouth open in astonishment. He commented that all my old aggression had disappeared and that my face looked totally different.

Having finished my course at the School of Acts Andrea and I began to think about what the future held for us. We knew we wanted to get a house of our own together and to have a baby, so we began to look around for a place of our own. More invitations began to come to minister back into the prison community and I could see the beginnings of what God would have me do for Him long term. I was invited back to HMP Channings Wood in Devon, to the very same therapy unit I had attended. I was delighted and decided to take Andrea with me. This was, I thought, just a visit rather than an opportunity to minister, but I was wrong. When we arrived at the place we spent quite a while sitting in the office chatting to the staff, who were amazed at the transformation that had taken place in me and couldn't believe how much I had changed. While we talked, 130 prisoners had been gathered together and, unbeknown to me, were waiting for me to come and speak to them. "Would you be willing to give a talk?" one of the officers asked me. "Yes, when?" I replied. "Now!" he said. So I went in, totally unprepared. I discovered that an overview of my story had been written up and had been posted on the notice board for the previous three weeks, so everyone knew who I was and knew a bit of my story. I shared my story with them and told them that the reason I had managed to get through the rehab programme was because of my faith in Jesus. I preached the Gospel to them and at the end of the talk many came forward to talk to me more about my faith. Since that first occasion I have had invitations from many other prisons and have gone in to share my testimony with others. It's ironic that previously I spent all my time trying to avoid the police, the court system, and stay out of prison. Now I spend a lot of my time working with the police, the court system, and trying to get into prisons!

During our time at Riverside Church Andrea and I became great friends with another couple, Shane and Lorraine Dean, who attended the same house group as us. At the time Shane was John Partington's assistant. Riverside belongs to the Assemblies of God group of Pentecostal churches and from time to time pastoral posts would come through to the office which Shane would look at and pass on to others as appropriate. Shane heard of a church in Weston-super-Mare that needed a new pastor and, at first, passed on the details to a few people he thought might be interested in the position. But information about the job kept landing back on his desk until he realized that God might be telling him he should take up the post himself. How that came to pass is a story in itself, but eventually Shane applied for and got the job. After he had been in this new post three or four months he knew that he needed help urgently and got in touch with me, suggesting I might be able to assist him.

By that time Andrea and I had our own house. It was something we'd longed for and so the decision to move was not one to be taken lightly. There would be no huge salary in Weston; it would be a faith venture if we decided to take it on. But after praying about it for some time, God spoke to Andrea and me separately about saying "yes" to Shane's offer and we knew it was right to give up our house and go. As if to confirm the matter further, when we put our house on the market God arranged a cash buyer and the house was sold in twenty-four hours! Having made the decision, in no time at all we found ourselves in Weston living in Shane and Lorraine's loft while we searched for a place to rent.

Today I am the assistant pastor of "H Church" in Weston-super-Mare, working alongside Shane, and taking special responsibility for the youth (as well as handling the many other things that crop up in a busy, thriving church in the midst of change). I am privileged to be able to minister in local prisons and I lead teams of young people in evangelistic outreaches in the town. Another programme I run is taking young people from the church to do gardening for disabled or older people who can't do it themselves. Andrea and I are renting a house that is located two minutes from the city centre in what is reputed to be the centre of drug dealing in Weston. Weston has the highest number of drug rehab institutions in the whole of the UK. I know that God has placed us here for a reason. We are reaching out to the broken people whose lives are being ravaged by drugs and who turn to crime to sustain their habits; to see them healed and put on the right path – the path towards Christ. I was once one of their number. Now God in His mercy is using me to rescue others. Glory to God!

Epilogue

The freedom I now have is something that is hard to explain and can only be experienced when you receive Jesus Christ as your Lord and Saviour. From reading the Bible I now understand that I am a "Kingdom carrier" and that part of Heaven lives in me through the Holy Spirit – the same power that raised Jesus from the dead. Jesus has given me power to live by, authority over the devil and a mission to fulfil which is to reach out to the lost at any cost. Now when I see someone who is living his or her life in and out of prison, trapped in a cycle of crime and drugs, or someone sleeping in a doorway, I get angry at the devil for ruining his or her life. I want to see every person come into the same relationship with Jesus that I have and be healed and helped out of their circumstances – to get their lives on the right track. My heart burns with a desire to see every person who is hurting and broken come to Jesus. Even now, as I write this, I know that there is someone somewhere trying to hit a vein with a fix of heroin; I know right now there are prostitutes selling their bodies to men for money to buy drugs; there are people in prison who are hurting so much that they are contemplating suicide. My heart burns to see them come to know God because I have tasted the truth and am now living it. I cannot keep silent with the message of freedom that God has given me and many others. This is what drives me. I don't need any other transient buzzes, only to tell others I was very lost, but now I am found.

Mark Rowan can be contacted via H Church at the following address:

> H Church
> Hughenden Road
> Milton
> Weston-super-Mare
> Somerset
> BS23 2UR

Or by email:

> info@hchurch.co.uk